FROM
ORPHAN
TO
Greatness

An African Story

Dear Michelle,
It truly was my Great Honor
to meet you.
Please stay Happy!

PIERRE KOMI T. ADADÉ

Sincerely,

Pierre K. T. Adadé
- Author -

PAGE PUBLISHING, INC.
Conneaut Lake, PA

First originally published by Page Publishing 2020

ISBN 978-1-6624-3039-8 (pbk)
ISBN 978-1-6624-3040-4 (digital)

Printed in the United States of America

Preface

It's nine twenty-two (Michigan time) this morning of March 8, 1994 (2:22 p.m. Togo time). I have decided to start putting in writing all the good and bad (mostly good) memories that I have about my mom and dad, memories as fresh in my mind as what I had for breakfast this morning. These memories, including those of my childhood, are still vivid, even though I haven't seen my family in nearly six years. I have been living, studying, and working in Kalamazoo, Michigan, and they are in my home village of Agadji, which is sixty miles northwest of Lome, the capital of Togo, a small French-speaking country in West Africa.

There comes a time in life when we take a short break from our daily routines and reach out to do something to make someone else's day a little brighter.

Not too long ago, that time came in my life. I stopped and decided to put together these words as a fulfillment of promise to my dear father.

I'm very thankful to the almighty good Lord, our creator, who has given me my family. While I am thankful for my siblings, Pauline, Fidel, and Jeanne, I am grateful almost beyond expression for my father, Mr. Adade Koffi Edoh, Alifa Otio Igneza Nicolas, and my mother, Mrs. Adade-Doumessi Akouwa Agbave Elizabeth. These two have been the most influential people in my life. With their unique personalities and drawing from their own life experiences, they made me who I am today.

Everyone's life circumstances come to them by chance. Some have it made; unfortunately, my parents, especially my father, have endured many hardships in their lives, but their sufferings have made them the strong, successful people they are now.

Many times when I was growing up in the small farming community of Agadji, in Togo, West Africa, I listened to my dear father recount stories from his life—so many times, in fact, that I decided to one day put them into writing as my way of showing respect to my father and, more importantly, to share my father's stories with others who may learn from them the way my siblings and I have.

All his life, my father has done everything he could to help his children succeed. As he likes to tell us, "My main goal in life is to help you succeed whatever the cost so you won't have to suffer the way I did. I wasn't fortunate enough to have someone help me." Yes, indeed, his life story has been full of tough experiences that bring him to tears whenever he talks about them. My father lost both his parents before the age of two. Thankfully, he was blessed by several miracles that saw him through those hard times.

Many parents in Agadji did not care much about their children's future, especially in terms of education. My father, however, since our first days in school, has always stood by us, seeing that we received a good education, found a good job, and enjoyed life.

Part of the reason for this was that as a little boy, my father had dreamed of going to school and becoming a doctor or a lawyer, but he never had a chance. Instead, he became first a tailor and then a farmer. After my father got married and he and my mother started having children, his dream became to have at least one of his children educated in an English-speaking country, like neighboring Ghana. Ghana held special memories for him because it was there, after spending ten years as an apprentice tailor, that he fell in love with Ghanaian culture and the English language, which he found more attractive than the French spoken in his native Togo. However, my father did not have enough money to send one of his children to study in Ghana or any English-speaking country, so the dream waited.

This dream of my father's seemed to have no chance of coming true until August 1981 when our Adade family was fortunate to meet one of the nicest American Peace Corps volunteers named Tom Edward Buchanan. Tom first became a fast friend of our family and then a full member during the next three years. When he left Togo in 1983 at the end of his Peace Corps assignment, Tom E. Buchanan never promised us he would return, but he kept in his heart a secret conviction to come back someday, which he did.

In June 1985, during that two-week visit, Tom E. Buchanan, friendly as ever, brought with him a retired American couple, Verne and Margaret Berry of Kalamazoo, Michigan. They were good friends of Tom who had grown tired of hearing him tell his incredibly nice stories about his African family, the Adades, so Verne and Margaret had decided to check things out for themselves and planned their first African trip to Togo to meet this family.

During that two-week visit, our visitors stayed in Agadji with us the whole time, and we did not let our Adade-Buchanan brother down. The Berrys left Togo reassured that the Adades were indeed everything that Tom E. Buchanan had led them to believe—a poor but nice, decent, respectful, and very respected family.

This visit of our valuable guests, Tom and the Berrys, which began somewhat casually, was to mark the beginning of the fulfill-ment of my father's long-held dream—that of having one of his chil-dren educated in an English-speaking country.

Tom E. Buchanan went on to land a job with USO and was given a position in Rome, Italy, where my older brother, Fidel, and myself had the honor and privilege to visit and travel around that beautiful country with him.

By the spring of 1989, Tom found himself reassigned to Frankfurt, Germany, as the executive director of USO. It was at this time that Tom made a move to show his appreciation to his Adade family for having taken such a good care of him during his Peace Corps years by arranging for me to transfer from the University of Benin in Lome, Togo, to Kalamazoo Valley Community College (KVCC), Kalamazoo, Michigan. In Kalamazoo, I would have a chance to learn about American culture and meet more American people whom the entire Adade family, including myself, were just crazy about. At the time, Tom was not aware that he was doing more than just helping my father raise one of his children but that he, in fact, was making one of my father's dearest dreams come true.

Because Tom was still living in Frankfort as we were making the arrangements for my trip to Kalamazoo, he contacted the always friendly and warm Verne and Margaret Berry, who agreed to give me room and board at their beautiful historic home on Elm Street in Kalamazoo. From the time I began my studies at KVCC until I graduated with an Associate of Arts degree in International Studies and Political Science on December 12, 1992, I lived with and shared great times and fun stories with Verne, Margaret, and James Berry, one of their five children. I have many fond memories of that time.

In addition to Tom E. Buchanan and Verne and Margaret Berry, who made it possible for me to be sitting in front of this computer typing these lines today, I would like to express my appreciation to people and friends who have helped me enjoy my American journey. These include the entire Berry family, Jim Dexeimer, Tommy and Greg, Mary and Karen, Russ and Weslie Tomlin, Jennie Springman, Mike and Pat Buchanan, Jack and Cathie Wolfgram, Mike and Debbie Wolfgram, Pat Buchanan, Steve and Alisa Lincoln and their family, and Dan and Kelly Laumers and their family.

My sincere appreciation to Su Cutler, one of the best instructors at KVCC, whose tremendous assistance helped me put these writings together.

A special thanks goes out in memorial to former US President John F. Kennedy whose idea to help poor nations around the world led to the creation of the Peace Corps program that gave me the incredible opportunity to live in this sweet country of freedom and democracy, the United States of America.

Above all, special thanks goes to my parents and the almighty God, my creator through whom everything came about.

This writing is mainly about Mom and Dad, not necessarily because they are my parents but because these two individuals who, by chance or mistake, gave birth to myself and my siblings and who have been and will always be the most influential persons in my life.

In this writing, I'll be reviewing my parents' childhoods to show why I think they are special and why I think I'm very lucky to have them for parents.

Chapter 1

TO MY FATHER

If we could make a wish before we were born and select our future family, I have no doubt that we would all share the wish to be born into a loving, caring family. Furthermore, I believe we all would wish to have kind, healthy parents who would be there whenever we needed them.

A third wish might be to be born into a family that was, while not rich, at least financially stable. I am equally sure that no one, especially no unborn baby, would ever wish to grow up as an orphan.

Imagine, if you will, for a moment a child born into a poor family who loses both parents before turning three. Think how unfair life would be to this child and how tough growing up would be for this innocent.

An orphaned child born in the United States has a far better chance of surviving than does a child born in a Third World country such as Togo. In Togo, under normal circumstances, a child struggles to make it past the age of five; this was especially true during the early 1900s when my father was born.

This unfortunate situation helps explain why polygamy and high birth rates have been part of life in many parts of the world. As no one could guarantee how many children would make it to adulthood, families had as many children as possible, hoping that one or two of them would survive, and more than one wife giving birth helped increase the number of children who might survive.

One child born into the difficult condition of being orphaned early was my father, who was born on a Friday in 1922 in the small village of Agadji in Togo, West Africa. At his birth, he was named Adade Koffi Nicolas; over his lifetime, his name grew with him until now he is known as Adade Koffi Nicolas Otio Igneza Edoh and Alifa.

The exact month and day on which my father was born was not recorded for two reasons. First, in our Akposso tribe, child's birthdate is not as important as the day of the week on which he or she is born; the latter is important because it determines a child's name.

Second, seventy-two years ago, when my father was born, birth certificates, driver's licenses, and passports were unheard of. Everyone knew everyone. Life was simpler. People didn't travel much. As a result, a person really didn't need to know his or her date, month, or even year of birth because no one had to prove when or where they had been born. With an increase in Western influence, which requires, even more, paperwork and greater movement and mixing of people, more records are being kept.Still, the majority of people my father's age know only their day of birth. The following is a list of possible tribal names based on the day of the week a child is born.

Weekday	Male	Female
Monday	Kodjo/Koudjo	Adjuwa/Adjo/Adjovi
Tuesday	Komla/Komlan	Abla/Ablavi
Wednesday	Kokou/Kouakou	Akoua/Akuwa/ Akouvi
Thursday	Yao/Yaovi	Yawa/Yawavi
Friday	Koffi/Kofi	Afi/Afiwa
Saturday	Komi/Kwame	Ame/Ama
Sunday	Kossi/Kwuassi	Kossiwa/Akossiwa

Though for some reasons my Akposso tribe does not have traditional names for some multiple births such as triplets, quadruplets or more, the Akposso tribe does have traditional names for twins, based on their gender and their order of birth.

Male	and	Female
Atsu/Atsou		Atsupé/Atsoupé
Male	**and**	**Male**
Atsu/Atsou (1rst born).		Outcha/Utcha (2nd born)
Female	**and**	**Female**
Oukoué/Ukué (1rst born).		Wassè/Wasseh (2nd born).

My father's name is Koffi because he was born on a Friday.

Nicolas was added to my father's name with his baptism into the Catholic Church; Igneza, his African traditional name, meaning "God gives life"; Otio is a nickname that his friends gave him. In fact, my father is very well known in Amou county by his unique nickname, Koffi-Otio. In a tribe like mine where there are all a lot of Koffis, Kossis, and Kokous due to their day of birth, it's a good idea for all to have a nickname as do many people in my village of Agadji.

Adade Alifa, my father's father, was from Agadji. My dad's mother, whose name was Oyai-Avani, was from the neighboring village of Amlame, about five miles away. She had two daughters, Adjoua and Atougbo, during her first marriage before getting a divorce. Shortly after the divorce, she married my grandfather. They lived in Agadji where my father was born in 1922. Though my father was born a healthy child, his parents were not so fortunate. One year after his birth, my father lost his dad to natural causes. His father must be in his early fifties. Then about a year or so later, my father lost his dear mother as well—a very painful beginning to my father's life.

Many times I have wondered how in the world my father survived. Maybe he was lucky, maybe he was tough, maybe he was born to suffer and to fight for everything he wanted. Perhaps his birthplace gave him some of the strength he would need to survive.

According to legend, Agadji, our village, is where the founding fathers of all the surrounding villages came from, and because the Akpossos, our tribe, are hunters, in the past, hunters from all these villages were required to pay tribute to their forefathers by presenting them with the head of a large wild animal (for example, a deer, buffalo, elephant, or wild cat) anytime one was killed. These animal heads, offerings to be eaten by forefathers or their representatives, were used in traditional ceremonies. Because of this tradition, the ancestors' village, our village, became known as "the village of those who eat jaws," originally Aigladjini and later shortened to Agadji.

Furthermore, according to legend, among the founders of Agadji were my own ancestor, Chief Adade, and his two counselors, Mr. Otou and Mr. Enagbe. Perhaps my father drew strength from the fact that his family had been living in Agadji since its foundation in the 1800s.

In addition, I believe that my father's life was truly saved by the community lifestyle that we have in Africa. No matter how poor we are, we care for each other, we look after each other. In a small African village like Agadji, everybody knows everybody; one person's sorrows and joys are those of the entire village. A village is a community where a child is raised not only by his or her parents and relatives but by the entire village. Yes it takes a village to raise a child. For example, in the absence of a misbehaving child's parents, he or she can be disciplined or yelled at by concerned adult in the village who later report the incident to the child's parents.

A common scene I saw growing up and that I pray still exists today was seeing villagers perform acts of charity such as bringing firewood, water, grain, clothes, or money to neighbors in need, including the sick, mothers with newborns, handicapped individuals, or families who had lost a loved one. It was beautiful to watch men and women form their separate and equal small self-help cooperatives through which they shared the hard work on one another's farms.

Because of this supportive, community-based lifestyle, being poor in Africa is much easier than being poor in industrialized Western countries. For example, in the United States, the philosophy of individualism encourages the notion that people are personally and individually responsible for the way their lives turn out, and this fosters the belief that individuals should "pull themselves up by their own bootstraps" but what IF you don't even have a boot to begin with? In Western industrialized countries, people seem much less concerned about their neighbors. The scene of countless homeless people living on city streets results from this lack of involvement with one another and is heartbreaking to members of my Akposso tribe. In addition, we find it very difficult to understand adult children who put their elders, especially their parents, in nursing homes and never go see them or see them only on rare occasions; children who talk disrespectfully to their elders and go unpunished by the older ones; wealthy people who only care about making more money; and this sorry list, unfortunately, goes on. It seems that selfishness and separateness have become a way of life in Western industrialized countries.

Luckily, a supportive community lifestyle existed when my father was orphaned, as it contributed to his survival. Part of this life-style includes a very broad definition of family, so few were surprised when, shortly after the death of his mother from untreated malaria, Adjuwa, the older of his two half-sisters from his mother's first marriage, took him under her care and moved him to Amlame. My dad was only two years of age at the time. My dad's sister's decision to take care of her brother was heroic and admirable, as she was only a young teenager herself. Some did think she was too immature to care for her little baby brother, or even to care for herself.

However, to the astonishment of villagers, Adjuwa successfully took good care of her baby brother. She even spoiled him.

My father's stories of the time he spent as a two-yearold with his older sister, Adjowa, are few. He has often told us that Adjowa took him with her everywhere she went.

Because Adjowa's father refused to send his daughters to school, she and sometimes my father's other sister, Atougbo, would spend all day playing with him, making sure he didn't cry. Another fond recollection of my father is that Adjowa would save her pennies and buy him a very sweet nonalcoholic palm wine called Tukumu that he loved. My dad also remembers that Adjowa would carry him on her back and rarely let him walk for fear that he might fall and hurt himself or get dirty. Needless to say, Adjowa always made sure her brother Koffi was well fed, washed, and wore clean clothes. Adjowa clearly took a great pleasure taking care of her brother and consequently was not prepared to lose custody of him.

When my father was about four, an uncle from Agadji decided to take him into his care and alleviate the now sixteen or so year old girl of the burden. Even though I think my dad's uncle acted properly, his sister Adjuwa was very unhappy. She was so attached to her baby brother that caring for him was never a burden to her. In fact, for Adjowa, having her baby brother taken away from her was the most horrible thing that could happen to her. It was ripping from her one of the last best things she had to call her own after the sudden death of her and my father's mother.

On the morning that my dad was being taken away, once it was clear to Adjowa that my father's uncle Edoh Koumodji was dead serious, she nearly injured herself. Throwing herself on the ground, she cried her eyes out and tried to steal her brother back by pulling him out of my dad's uncle's hands, but she sadly lost the battle. Well, as a young teenager fighting an older man, her father's age, how could she have won?

Still, because she was a strong older sister whose best wish was to see her brother make it through life, even though Adjowa could no longer care for her poor little brother directly, she refused to stop loving him and kept caring for him as much as she could from a distance. Every Sunday after attending her Protestant church, she came to Agadji, usually alone and sometimes with her younger sister, Atougbo, to spend a happy hour or two with their brother Koffi.

Let me pause here to congratulate Africans and all other people who value community life. Life is very painful when we don't live together in harmony. Why do we make life more painful than it needs to be by hating one another instead of helping out? Thanks to that deep sense of community life in my country Togo and in Africa as a whole, my dad had a family. Anything short of that deep belief in community life would have forced my dad's family to give him up for adoption or send him to an orphanage. I'm not trying to criticize the institution of adoption or orphanages. I'm simply saying that thanks to our style of community life, my father was kept among his own people. Thanks to that same lifestyle, I myself and my siblings have a father, a mother, and, above all, a family, one of the most feared and respected in Agadji.

Did I say that my father was at times spoiled by his sister in Amlame? That is right. My dad, like any child, loved the sweets and sweet times with his sister. Unfortunately, when his uncle Koumodji Edoh from Agadji took custody of him, my father's sweet days were over: they all disappeared from his life at the age of four.

Like the vast majority of people in West Africa, My dad's uncle Edoh was a hardworking farmer and hunter. Farming is very hard work in our country where everything has to be done by hand.

However, the hardest part is that the income from farming only comes in once a year. Crops such as corn, beans, peanuts, and millet are widely grown, but there is hardly enough grown to feed the family and there is little left to sell and raise cash for the family.

One reason for both polygamy and having many children in farming communities is so that each family will have more manpower to farm more land and bring in a larger harvest.

The living cost in rural community is very low; as a result, a farmer can spend very little on his children but get a lot of work out of them.

The results can also be unpredictable, as farming relies totally on the weather. The better the weather, the better the harvest. Unfortunately, weather betrays farmers in many ways. The rain sometimes comes too early or too late. It may rain too hard on the crops, or it may simply rain too much or too little. Crops also need steady but calm breezes to encourage them to grow normally, but if the wind is too strong, it can destroy them. The sun is also needed in the development of crops; unfortunately, that same sun can burn them if it's too hot. Farmers closely watch nature and the colors of the sky with all fingers crossed.

Farming is a gambling profession that keeps a good farmer on alert day in and day out. When the harvest is good, families do just fine, both food- and money-wise. When the harvest is bad, not only do the families eat up the grains saved in the silos in a matter of weeks, but they also seriously feel the pinch financially.

Farmers' problems would be somewhat alleviated if they could practice farming techniques, such as irrigation, using oxen, etc. Unfortunately, for the most part, these techniques are not used in traditional farming systems in Africa.

*****

Uncle Edoh was in his late sixties and had only one son who was named Komlan because he had been born on a Tuesday. Komlan was six or ten years older than my father. Even though my dad's uncle liked him a lot, it didn't take my father long to realize that his new half-brother, Komlan, was, and would always be, the favorite.

Back in those years, Western-style education had already begun to bear some of its best fruits. The Western-educated generation was already entering a different kind of work, which was totally unlike farming and had been known for generations. These educated "youngsters" started working as clerks for the government and doing many other Western-style jobs based on their education level. And they were paid monthly—a radical concept! The idea of having a monthly income instead of a yearly one from farming was very appealing to my father's uncle's generation, so much so that it became very fashionable for parents of his age to send their children, mostly males, to school so that they could get educated and find a monthly income job in a nearby city, often the capital city of Lome.

The goal was for these educated children to, in return, assist their parents and other family members financially.

Under that social pressure, parents who could send their male children to school did so quickly, while those who could not accept the fact that they had no choice but to keep their children on the farm and enjoy their physical help. In many polygamist families, the father was financially unable to send all his male children to school, so if the idea of "sending my sons to school" became popular among the concubines or wives of one man, there would begin a competition, a struggle that only the most influential and most liked wives won.

My father had to deal with this type of situation. Unfortunately, my father had nobody to speak for him. He had already lost his parents and been forced to live with his uncle. His uncle and his wife had a son of their own who was older than my father. While his uncle tried to treat them equally, clearly Komlan was spoiled by his mother, my dad's new stepmother. At first, they both went to school. Komlan was in the sixth grade at the time my dad started first grade.

Two years after my father was moved into his uncle's house, due to the influence of his wife, my dad's uncle pulled him out of school, supposedly for financial reasons. Komlan was allowed to continue his education while my dad was forced to farm with his uncle. Once again, my dad, now at the age of seven, had to swallow a bitter pill.

The experience taught my father a tough lesson: life is not fair. *How can such a thing happen to a poor seven-year-old orphan like me?* he would ask. Who was there to answer such a heartbreaking question? Nobody. Nobody but God our Creator, who, for some reason known only to him, had decided not only to make my dad an orphan but also to give him these difficult experiences.

However, my father always met his difficulties head-on. So the first morning, following Mr. Edoh's decision to pull my dad out of school, my dad, without any resistance, got ready to go farm with his uncle. He never returned to school.

This was the beginning of a journey into a totally new adventure and experience, one he would travel his entire life—farming. Today my father is still a farmer and a very successful one. Successful does not necessarily mean wealthy, which, as a matter of fact, he is not. Still, despite his success, my dad says that if he had been given a choice between education and farming, he would have chosen to continue his schooling.

*****

In addition to the care he received from his living relatives, I think that though my dad's parents were dead, they continued to give their young son physical, emotional, and psychological strength to survive. They never ceased to watch over and protect their child from whom death had stolen them. They were always next to him, crying and laughing with him. I strongly believe these things happen, as does everyone in my village, for in my tribe, we believe the dead do not leave the living; rather, they watch over the loved ones they leave behind.

In my tribe, we also believe that the dead can answer prayers, so we must always be careful what we ask for. This is a lesson we young Adades learned from my aunt Ovi's experience. It was an experience I witnessed myself.

I was twelve and living with my family in my home village Agadji on the day that Aunt Ovi, one of my favorite father's side aunts, passed away, but let us begin where Aunt Ovi's misery started— shortly after she returned to Agadji following a failed marriage. For more than fifteen years, she had been married to Mr. Ankou, a truck driver. Aunt Ovi, her husband, and their three daughters had lived a relatively happy life in the city of Atakpame, twenty miles from Agadji, until Mr. Ankou decided to divorce Aunt Ovi for a younger woman.

With no other place to turn to, Aunt Ovi moved back to her own village with her daughters and eventually became a farmer like many others in the village. Though Aunt Ovi and her daughters received a warm welcome home from her relatives and she managed to transition from being a housewife living in the city to being a farmer and a single mother of three living in a tiny village, her happiness did not last long.

When Aunt Ovi first moved back to Agadji, she lived right across from our home. She was one of the sweetest aunts my siblings and I had. She loved to sing to us whenever she was in good mood; she also tried with all her heart to rescue us so many times from our parents when we got ourselves in trouble and were about to be disciplined. About 97 percent of the time, her attempts failed, but she never gave up. She really loved my father and his young family, and we also cared a lot for her in return.

Soon, the reality of life in a small village, with its poverty and petty arguments with neighbors and relatives, started taking its toll on her.

Aunt Ovi's real problem with depression didn't start until after she moved four houses down from us, remarried, and had another daughter named Adjo. At least twice a week, we would find Aunt Ovi in tears despite her efforts to keep her happy nature alive. It became apparent that Aunt Ovi was going through some tough times. My father, her favorite cousin, helped her out as much as he could by listening to her problems, giving her advice, supplying her with farm goods, and assisting her financially; unfortunately, all this seemed to make little difference.

Aunt Ovi's feelings were easily hurt. One day, she almost cried her eyes out during an argument with her cousin, Komlan, my father's half brother. I'm sure that day Komlan was trying to impress his cousin Ovi, with whom he was arguing when he asked in his illiterate broken English,

"What do you mean?" My poor aunt Ovi must have felt as if she had been insulted in that foreign language that she didn't understand, and she was reduced to tears. Only my father was able to convince her that what her cousin Komlan had said was not an insult, but no matter how he had said it. Aunt Ovi could not see the end of the tunnel for her misery. One morning, she did something unheard of. In my Akposso tribe, we perform a traditional ceremony called a libation during which we ask our ancestors or dead relatives for only two kinds of help—blessings and protections, nothing else, However, that morning, when Aunt Ovi was giving a libation to her dead older brother named Zogidi, instead of asking for his protection, she asked him, in tears, to come and take her with him, away from her misery, because her life was not worth living anymore. If Aunt Ovi had given the matter deep thought, she might have guessed that her dead brother, Zogidi, was well aware of her pains and had just been waiting for her to call him to her rescue.

Two or three days after Aunt Ovi's libation, she became ill. It started out like a normal illness, but soon the entire family was worrying about her situation, and even before the family had a chance to raise money to take her to the hospital in Atakpame, our dear Aunt Ovi passed away, leaving behind her husband, their one-year-old daughter, Adjo, and her three teenage daughters.

*****

Even though my father's parents watched over him, they could not make his life easy for him. Due to his early experiences, my father, at the ripe of eight, understood that the five fingers of one's hands are not equal—some are shorter than others and some skinnier. Likewise, he understood that some people are born poor, others rich; some privileged, others underprivileged. At this very young age, he had been forced to understand that if one wants to achieve, one must work hard.

While his earliest years were difficult to endure, it is probable that my father is the wonderful, hardworking person he is today because of those experiences. Throughout his whole life, my father has tried to excel in whatever he has undertaken. He is always eager to compete and to do his best; he loves challenge. In addition, my father does not have one iota of jealousy toward anybody who has been successful; instead, he learns from them, using them as his role models, his challengers. My dad is always content with what he has and never tries to have anything beyond his means.

This personality trait existed even at the age of eight; therefore, instead of being mad at his uncle for putting an end to his education, my dad embraced his new destiny with open arms and a warm heart. While, in truth, he did not have any other option, his positive attitude was remarkable in one so young.

His attitude helped him to accept whatever duties he was given, so while household morning activities, such as doing dishes, were usually done by the females of the family, because my father was the youngest child on his dad's side of the family and because there was no girl in the family, he was the one who had to do the female work. Therefore, in his new life as a farmer, every morning before sunrise, he was on his feet doing chores, such as washing dishes from the previous night's dinner and sweeping the living quarters, kitchen, and entire compound. It wasn't until after those early morning chores that he was allowed to have a breakfast of dinner's leftovers. After having worked for two or three good hours, he would then be ready to go to the fields. You might say my father's life was like that of Cinderella in the fairy tale only my father would have to find his own way out of the situation.

*****

In the West, most family activities, especially activities such as using the restroom or doing dishes, are done inside the house. For my father, dishes, laundry, and cooking were all done outside, and a trip to the restroom was a good distance from the house, somewhere in the nearby bushes. Showers were taken around the corner of a house at a specific location.

Because all these activities took place outside the house in the "compound" or yard, the area was kept as clean as possible. Every morning between five thirty and seven o'clock and every evening before dark, wives and their children would be busy sweeping the compound with special brooms made out of coconut or palm tree leaves. While the sweepers usually stopped at the edge of the compound, they might sweep their neighbors' compounds as well, especially in the case of an illness or when the neighbor was gone on a trip.

After sweeping the compound, as the day became brighter, my father would turn his attention to the dishes from the previous night, which had piled up to be saved till morning. Unlike in the big cities where average citizens enjoy the luxuries of modern living, such as running water, telephone, and electricity, these are nonexistent in the villages.

In villages, petroleum lanterns and stove fires are the sources of light, and these are not cheap, as only a few people can afford more than two lanterns. In fact, a family's economic level is still measured by the number of lanterns in the household; the better off a family is financially, the more lanterns they will have, and a truly well-to-do family might afford enough petroleum to light the compound throughout the night.

The average cost of petroleum is about fifty cents per gallon. For the average villager in Togo who only makes about $75 yearly, that fifty cents, the equivalent of 150 CFA francs (the currency under the French franc used in most West African countries), was a lot of money; therefore, nighttime use of lanterns was limited, and lanterns were used only for the most important purposes, such as keeping a light next to a newborn baby, cooking supper, or letting children study.

In my tribe, there is a strong separation of duties between husband and wife, between older and younger sisters, between older and younger brothers, and, above all, between males and females. For example, the father is always responsible for the happiness of the entire family by working hard every day and putting food on the table. The father does not cook meals and does dishes. The mother's responsibility is to make sure the family is fed; she does dishes and laundry, buys groceries, and stays home most of the time to watch the children.

Duties on both sides are designed so that a husband and a wife respect each other for their contribution to the wellbeing of the family. The arrangements also includes making certain that each person is fulfilling his or her duties. Often society itself is there as a watchdog to make sure not only that husbands and wives are playing the roles they should but also that lines are not being crossed. For instance, a wife who tries to take over her husband's duties is regarded by society as "an ugly tomboy" and ridiculed.

I have one of those tomboys in my own family, and her name is Massa. Massa, a close cousin, is the daughter of Mr. Zogidi, my aunt Ovi's dead brother. At a very young age, Massa was known in the entire village for her extraordinary strength and stubbornness. The youngest of three, Massa was still very young when both her parents died, and she was raised by her aunt on her father's side. At a very young age, as in my father's situation, Massa lived through some tough situations that helped make her strong; in fact, she can perform almost any physical task that a man can.

Massa was different in other ways as well. Though she went to and graduated from elementary school, she never, like many girls her age, attended college. Massa was never a member of any social group such as the Akpe group or the village choir like many of her friends. Furthermore, Massa was the last girl of her age group to begin dating; in fact, she didn't start until her early thirties and then only to a divorced older man named Ankou, who, maybe because of his age and experience, was tough enough to handle her. Other than Ankou, Massa never seriously attracted any man in the village. While it may be true that this was partly because she was not very attractive, mostly, I think, it was because she scared the men away because of her stubbornness and being a tomboy.

Though Massa loves kids, she has never had any of her own. Some people blame her childlessness on her "tomboy" status, suggesting that she is too macho to be fertile.

According to these people, Massa would have to change and relax more to become fertile, but Massa has never learned any other way of approaching life other than as who she is—a very strong woman, the perfect tomboy.

The same kind of mockery is applied to men or husbands who try to take over their wives' or girlfriends' duties by cooking too often, doing dishes, or especially by grocery shopping. These men are made fun of by everyone in society, including those same women that they are supposedly helping. These men are labeled as "stingy" because it is said they want to keep for themselves money left from the groceries.

I still remember those unpleasant comments that people made about a male cousin named Godwin. Godwin was three or four years older than my older sister, Pauline. Not only was he a close cousin of ours, but his family home was only one house down from ours.

Like my cousin Massa, Godwin was not a very attractive man. Also, like Massa, Godwin never belonged to any social groups, but unlike Massa and many others, Godwin was very smart and did very well in school. He passed all the school's toughest exams. The oldest of five, early on he took his responsibility as a leader in his family seriously. To many parents, including my own, he was the perfect child because he did not believe in drinking or partying. My mother has always been best friends with Godwin's mother, Amavi, who is, by the way, one of my favorite aunts. Many times my mother would ask Fidel and myself to follow our cousin Godwin's example by studying hard and doing well in school.

Godwin was unpopular as well. He loved to perform domestic tasks, including those socially set aside as female duties. The funny part was that Godwin never cared about the village gossip about him. True, Godwin did receive some positive comments from mothers in the village, who wished their sons would do as Godwin did; still, his behavior scared away potential girlfriends to whom Godwin represented a selfish, stingy young man who would not want to share with friends of the opposite sex.

Godwin went on and graduated from high school and later the University of Benin in Lome with a highly respected master's degree in Agriculture. Though Godwin did not have a girlfriend until he was almost through with school, he did finally manage to get married in his late thirties and now has several children.

*****

My dad quickly forgot what it was like to be in a classroom and started learning how to grow crops, especially coffee and cocoa.

My Akposso tribe lives in Southwestern Togo, near the border with Eastern Ghana. That region has the best soil for the planting of coffee and cocoa.

The southwestern part of Togo, also called the mountainous region where my father and later myself grew up, and the whole southern region stretching from the capital city of Lome located by the Atlantic Coast all the way to the city of Blita located in the central part of the country and going up north, has four seasons: one long and one short rainy season and one long and one short dry season. The region contains four counties (Kloto, Amou, Wawa, and Ogou) and is the only region where coffee and cocoa are grown.

Unlike the grassy vegetation found in the remaining part of the country, this mountainous region is covered by forests that were once full of wild animals, including a wide variety of monkeys, all kinds of birds, poisonous snakes, deer, antelope, and buffalos. Because the Akposso have always been hunters, these animals, with the exception of those who migrated to safer lands, have been wiped out. Though the mountainous region is not the place to look for Africa's breathtaking animals, as in Kenya in Eastern Africa, it remains a tourist attraction because of the terrain that is always alive with beautiful green vegetation, especially during the raining season, which lasts from the end of April to mid-October.

Perhaps most important to Togo today, the mountainous region produces 85 percent of Togo's delicious fruits for mostly in a country consumption. There is a wide variety of fruit, all big, juicy, and nice-looking, including bananas, oranges, sugarcanes, mangoes, pineapples, guavas, avocados, and lemons, only to name a few.

Togo, like most African countries, offers different vegetation and climates in different parts of the country. The northern part of the country is mostly dry and grassy with two seasons: a rainy and a dry one, each lasting six months. With its savannah-type vegetation, its major role in the nation's economy is that it provides land suitable for the planting of crops, such as corn, wheat, peanuts, and beans— all for in-country consumption. Cotton is also grown, but along with coffee and cocoa, it is used for export; together these three crops provide 60 percent of the nation's export revenues.

*****

Working in his uncle's coffee fields, it was not long before my dad started showing his uncle how devoted he was to his new occupation. Convinced that my dad would make a good farmer, his uncle started teaching him special techniques and farming secrets; this was done the way grandfathers give candies to their favorite and well-behaved grandchildren. As time went by, my father became very close to his uncle, so close that as his uncle was growing older and weaker, he made my father the heir to some of his farms.

At the same time, his uncle was deeply concerned and disappointed by his own spoiled son who spent his father's money on luxury, women, and parties instead of concentrating on his education. Two weeks before his death, my dad's uncle apologized to my dad for not sending him to school instead of his own son.

Shortly after the death of his uncle, my dad's half brother, Komlan, who had been living an extravagant life in the city instead of pursuing his education seriously, returned to his village to take up farming like my dad. It was obvious that Mr. Komlan made this decision because he had no other options. Unfortunately, for my father, his half brother came back as a failed, and therefore an angry, unhappy man, jealous of everything my dad had accomplished through his hard labor.

Having grown up in the village, my dad's half brother had many close relatives willing to back him up whenever there was a problem between him and my father. My dad's only close relative was his older half sister, Adjowa, living in Amlame and the sister who had raised him for a very short time. Because she was from a different village, she had neither authority nor influence with my dad's family in Agadji. As a result, many times my dad ended up the loser in arguments with his half brother.

Tired of being kicked around all the time, my dad decided to leave his village and go into temporary exile to find peace of mind. He decided to go to the neighboring country of Ghana, which used to be called the Gold Coast. Why Ghana? First of all, Ghana had long been the dream country to our villagers. Secondly, one of my father's distant relatives from Amlame was still in Ghana. Because this relative was a cousin of my father's sister, Adjuwa, and also because he did not want to make any final decision without checking with her first, he decided to go and discuss the idea with her.

Until this day, my father remembers that Sunday when very early in the morning he knocked at his sister Adjuwa's door in Amlame. It was a Sunday because Adjuwa and her husband, like all good farmers, loved to go to their farms early in the morning, Monday through Saturday, and my father knew he would have no chance on any other morning.

Adjuwa was very surprised to find her brother Koffi standing nervously at her doorstep that morning. "What is the matter?" she anxiously asked my father.

"Nothing, please calm down, sister," my father responded. "I know it's highly unusual for me to come to you at this early hour of the day, but like I said, calm down. It's nothing to worry about. I'm here to seek advice regarding a decision that I'm about to make."

"What is it?" Adjuwa interrupted, as if my father was not talking fast enough. "What is it?"

"You know, sister, I wish I could be happier in my village of Agadji, but I'm not. I'm honestly, getting tired of the little arguments that I've been having lately with my relatives there. I'm tired of the unfair treatment that I've been getting from those relatives that I love and respect. Before these little arguments become major ones, I'm thinking about leaving my village for a couple of years in order to let the tensions cool off a little. As you know, I've always wanted to live in Ghana. From what I've heard, Ghana is doing very well economically and socially compared to our Togo. Maybe I will be happier in Ghana than I am at this moment."

Surprised but secretly pleased with her brother's speech, Adjuwa paused for a short moment and asked, "So tell me. What will your relatives in Agadji think about this? What will happen to your uncle's farm? What will—"

Before Adjuwa even finished her question, my father cut her short. "Please don't worry about all that. As far as I'm concerned, some of them will be happy to see me go. Like I said, I'll only be gone for a couple of years, and who knows, if things don't turn out well for me and I'm still alive, I may return home sooner."

Adjuwa became sad upon hearing that statement from her brother and was about to start crying when, as if to console her, he asked, "Tell me. Did you say you have a cousin who lives in Ghana? What is his name again? Hmmm, I forgot. Hmmm."

Before my father could remember the name, his sister, enlightened by the suggestion, interrupted, "Yeah," she said, "Dete Tchoto! That's right! Dete will love to have you with him in Ghana. He is single with no children. That is right!"

The conversation shifted from Adjuwa's worries to strategies to make her brother Koffi's wishes come true. Before the conversation was over that morning, Adjuwa had come up with a plan to make it possible for her brother to join her cousin Dete in Ghana, who, as my father correctly pointed out, was doing better on every level than Togo.

Ghana's advancements were due, among other things, to the political system adopted by the British colonizers, a political system known as the indirect rule, far different in strategy from the direct rule used by the French colonizers in Togo. The direct rule system used by the French in their colonies throughout the world stripped the indigenous peoples of their cultures, their ways of thinking, their ways of solving problems; in short, the system took away from them whatever made them who they were. Through the direct rule, French was imposed on the indigenous peoples as their new national language; education in French was mandatory, and tribal languages were banned from schools. The territorial French governors got their orders directly from France. The orders were carried out by governors, who ruled with an iron fist, and their regional appointees.

With direct rule, the social structures of villages collapsed as quickly as a castle in a strong wind built on a sand dune in the Sahara desert. Every aspect of traditional life was neglected. Village chiefs who had played a major role in solving problems between families were stripped of their power or else quickly became puppets of the French government, and so they spent most of their time worrying about how to make the French government and its governors happy instead of worrying about the well-being of their people as they had done before colonization. These village chiefs spent their time collecting taxes, lumber, and palm oil for the French.

Education—that is, French education—was the only thing promoted and encouraged under the direct rule system; this was so that indigenous educated people could be employed by the French administration as clerks, policemen, and in other jobs.

For those whose parents had enough money to send them to the French schools, it was indeed wonderful to get an education and then a job. On the other hand, those who, like my father, could not go to school had a difficult time surviving. Unfortunately, there was not much for these individuals to do besides become farmers. Often these people became poor farmers and then unhappy, bitter people, and bitter people can cause trouble for others.

My dad's half brother was one of those bitter farmers, and my dad became a target for his half brother's frustration. As the situation became unbearable, my father's only real option was to leave. Hence, he was on his way to Ghana where he could live with his cousin Dete.

Though the decision for my father to leave could be interpreted as happening mostly for family reasons, the direct rule system of the French definitely contributed to the outcome. As did the fact that in Ghana, then called the Gold Coast, Great Britain used the indirect rule system, which allowed the indigenous peoples all kinds of freedom, such as freedom of speech (the indigenous peoples were allowed to openly disagree and criticize the government through the media), freedom of art (the indigenous peoples were allowed to develop and improve their art work and music), and freedom to speak their native languages, one of which, Ewe, eventually became written and used in schools.

Under an indirect rule administration, the culture and social structures of the indigenous peoples were maintained, reinforced, and encouraged from above. The traditional chiefs even maintained their power and high authority, and some became even more influential under the English.

As with the French, the British encouraged education. However, English was taught along with Ewe, one of the most widely spoken African languages in Ghana and Togo. In addition, the British government encouraged attendance at schools that provided practical training as well as those that provided higher liberal education through loans and financial assistance. The purpose of training schools was to provide an opportunity for advanced training in a trade. It is a great idea. Before long, the indirect rule system's training schools paid off; Ghanaians became shoemakers, cobblers, tailors, brick layers, masons, carpenters, mechanics, and other skilled tradesmen. As a result, the economy and the quality of life of ordinary people in Ghana began to improve.

Indirect rule has supported people in Ghana in keeping their rich, diverse cultures, and traditions and in improving their way of life. They have become innovators, developing special fabrics, such as kente cloth, and a form of music that I adore called "High Life."

During my father's time in the early '40s, Ghana was experiencing its Renaissance and attracting people from Togo and other West African countries. In fact, the Gold Coast was such an attractive place that everyone in Togo wanted to go there because, for people like my father who couldn't go to school, Ghana offered choices besides farming. Of course, moving to and trying to start life in a new place can be difficult.

Again, thanks to the extended family and a cousin in Ghana, my father had a way into the country. When Adjuwa contacted him, her cousin agreed to help my father and have him live with him in Ghana; after all, he and my dad were distantly related themselves.

My father left for Ghana on the morning of January 19, 1941, with another "uncle," another distant cousin through his sister, Adjuwa.

Adjowa did not give her brother a bon voyage party, not because she didn't want to but because she simply could not afford one. My father remembers standing on his sister's doorstep, exactly where a few days before he had stood to ask her advice. It was there that he left her sister in tears as they said goodbye.

Once again, there was a painful separation between Adjuwa and her brother. Their bond had grown stronger over the years, even though my dad had lived in Agadji. However, unlike their previous parting, Adjuwa felt at ease. Her brother was much older this time, and he was going to live with someone she knew very well and trusted. This time, Adjuwa was sure her dear younger brother would be well taken care of.

His uncle would travel with him to Ghana by foot. Because my father and his uncle Kodjo knew they were going to walk to Ghana, they carried with them only what they absolutely needed. My father had two shirts, two shorts, one bedsheet, and the clothes and shoes he was wearing. As far as food, they carried none. My father recalls drinking at the creeks they crossed during their journey and eating wild fruit along the way.

This long journey from our village to Hohoe in Ghana took them two long days by foot. The first day was the hardest—twelve hours of nonstop walking to Koute or Kute on the Togolese side of the border with Ghana. The second day was shorter, only six hours, after which they finally arrived in the mighty city of Hohoe. They walked partly because Adjuwa could not afford to send them to Ghana by bus and partly because public transportation in those years was very rare.

In Hohoe, as expected, my father's uncle Dete, a bricklayer and mason, was waiting for them and received them with an open heart and arms.

Uncle Kodjo did not stay in Hohoe long, just enough time to make sure that my dad and Dete were getting along well. Then he returned to Amlame to reassure Adjuwa of her brother's positive reception.

Soon my father and his uncle Dete became so close that my dad began calling him Fofo, meaning "older brother." To my father, calling his uncle "brother" was very meaningful. Perhaps my dad was trying to show his sadness for not having a true brother, or perhaps he was expressing his feelings that this distant uncle, instead of bossing him around, gave him the love and devotion of a real brother. True, my dad had a half brother back home whom he had tried to love, but he had only received hatred in return.

My dad's new Fofo was single and had no children, not because he didn't want any but because he suffered from epilepsy. Epilepsy and leprosy are diseases greatly feared by people in West Africa, especially in Togo and Ghana. These diseases are falsely considered highly contagious, and their victims are either kept away from society or, if allowed to stay, are denied what many view as natural opportunities in life, like getting married and having children.

My father and his uncle's relationship was one of mutual joy and satisfaction. While my dad desperately needed someone older to show him the way, his uncle needed a trustworthy companion. They found a special refuge in each other.

Shortly after Kodjo's departure, Uncle Dete Tchoto called my father to him one Sunday morning, made my dad sit down, and asked him why he had decided to come to Ghana.

"Koffi," Dete said to my father, "tell me what happened."

"Like we say in our Akposso tribe, as you know," my father started, "whenever you see a tortoise, a usually slow walking animal, going full speed or wild animals running in every direction, this means there is danger. This means there might be a wildfire coming their way."

*****

One of the things that I personally have come to love about African languages is their complexity. Languages in which the same word carries two, three, even four different meanings depending on how it is said. For instance, a click sound resulting from flapping the tongue against the lower part of the mouth in Akposso can mean yes, no, or be an insult depending on variation in the sound.

Likewise, the Akposso language has countless proverbs considered adult or sophisticated language. They can be used as a code to confuse a foreigner who happens to know some Akposso or to prevent youngsters from being fully exposed to adult discussions.

It was this manner of speech that my father was using.

Though only a teenager, my father opened his story with this proverb to give his uncle Dete a clear idea of his situation in Agadji. "I know you understand what I mean by this proverb, don't you?" my father asked quietly, as if to make sure that his uncle Dete hadn't lost his fluency in his native Akposso after all ten years in Ghana.

"Of course, I understand," Dete replied. "But," he continued, "I also want to hear all the little details, the whole story."

"Okay, okay," my father said and then paused to collect his thoughts before he continued. The proverb had set the stage, and then my father went on and told the unpleasant details of his life in Agadji. He made sure he did not leave out anything. He talked about his many little fights with his relatives in Agadji, especially with his half brother, Komlan, and concluded with his observation that life in Togo was becoming very hard because of the direct rule political system imposed by the French colonizers.

Though Dete did not like what he heard from my dad, he was relieved that my father had managed to leave Togo and come into his life. As if Dete wanted to put a smile on my father's face, he changed the subject and asked my dad what hobbies he liked to do. My father passionately told him about his love for soccer and his dream to someday play on a major league team in Togo or Ghana. To make the conversation complete, Dete told my father everything about his life, everything including information about his epilepsy.

"Well, as you can see, Koffi," Dete continued, "I'm not fortunate either to be living a rosy life in this foreign country. I'm just surviving but I am delighted to have you here, and believe me, together we are going to make something positive out of these depressing lives of ours. As we say in Akposso, 'One hand washes another.' We'll just have to make sure we are there for one another."

Totally satisfied with what he heard from his uncle, my father politely thanked him and vowed to be there for him through good and bad times. My father also decided from that day on to help his uncle with household chores, such as doing dishes and laundry, ironing clothes, buying groceries, and sweeping their home, in order to give Dete more time to concentrate on their financial situation.

After they had listened to each other's life stories, Mr. Dete decided to work and save money to send my father to a regular school where my father would have a chance to pursue general studies, eventually become a government clerk, and hold down a nice office job where he could make good money. My dad really liked the idea of going back to school and was ready to start right away, so Dete took my father to see the nearest elementary school principal who, because the school was coming to an end', advised they wait until after the recess. The principal asked Dete to come see him personally a week or two before the new school year started so that he could make sure that my father was enrolled.

Excited by this talk, Mr. Dete Tchoto, was even more motivated than before to save money and send my dad to school, and he did manage to save enough money for my father's tuition. Unfortunately, on the very eve of Dete's appointment with the school principal, which would have, without a doubt, led to my father's enrollment, his dear uncle Dete had a health crisis, and the school money had to be spent to pay for the hospital and the traditional medicine men in search of a treatment. During the six weeks that Dete was in the care of doctors and traditional medicine men, my father made himself into a nurse's aide, staying faithful to the promise he and his uncle Dete had made to each other.

By the time Dete was fully recovered from the crisis, he had not only spent all the money saved for my father's schooling but also gone into debt.

Because Dete's epilepsy usually resulted in a health crisis every one to three months, he knew it would happen again, so he and my father had a long serious talk. Mr. Dete advised my dad to forget going back to school and to learn a profession instead. He again pledged to my dad his financial support. My father's first thought was to become a shoemaker, but because he had a dream, he told his uncle he would become a tailor. He may have also known that the average Togolese spends more money on their clothes, which are sewn by a local tailor, than on repairing their shoes.

The morning after their discussion, my father's uncle took him to one of the most talented, best-known tailors in Hohoe. There my father faced a very tough situation—yes, another one. His new boss, whose name was Emmanuel Adjassey, already had fourteen apprentices.

Technically, fourteen was too many apprentices for one person to handle, but because of Mr. Emmanuel's good reputation, everybody in Hohoe and the surrounding towns who was interested in becoming a tailor wanted to learn from him. My dad didn't like the idea of becoming the fifteenth apprentice. He was afraid this master would not have time to instruct him. Plus, being the newest arrival, he would be bossed around by all the senior apprentices in a manner similar to the treatment that new recruits receive in the military or that pledges get when they join fraternities.

After a long talk between Mr. Emmanuel and Mr. Dete, the master tailor agreed to take my dad on under the condition that he spend two months on probation. During those two months, the boss would see if my father had the courage to learn the job and the ability to cope with being number 15. One third of the training fees would be due at the end of those two months. My father did not like the idea, but he did not have any choice but to settle for whatever offer he could get. At the same time, he was pleased that his long waiting period was coming to an end.

During the probationary period, my father was living with his uncle Dete. He would get up early every morning and do chores at home and then head to his boss's compound and perform the same tasks with the addition of cleaning the tailor shop before it opened for the day. Due to his good work ethics, my father earned the respect of the other apprentices. They were also impressed by him simply because he was a foreigner and, therefore, different.

When the two months were up and the time arrived to finalize the contract, my dad's uncle suffered another, even worse, health crisis. My father found himself having to care for his uncle and trying to fulfill his duties as an apprentice and satisfy his boss.

After three weeks in the hospital, Mr. Dete was even more determined to finalize the apprentice contract for his dear devoted nephew. After months of waiting, the contract was finally signed on a Monday morning in 1942. That day, my father and his uncle Dete took one poms and ten sillies (pom and silly are Ghanaian currency) and two bottles of Ghanaian beer to Mr. Emmanuel. The actual process only lasted an hour. Then exactly one week after the contract was signed, my father suffered another terrible blow—his uncle passed away.

Alone in his new country, despite obtaining the apprenticeship, my father felt a failure because he was unable to fulfill his traditional obligation to his uncle. Because of his poor financial situation, my father could not return his uncle's body to his home village of Amlame in Togo. Instead, my dad had to bury his uncle in Hohoe, the Ghanaian village where he died. This was only possible, thanks to the generous help of his uncle's good friends, who had come to cherish him during his years in Ghana.

My father was still a teenager when these changes occurred but not a typical one. He never had the chance to relax and enjoy his teenage years; he never learned how to have fun; he never went to movies, bars, or even on a date. He just didn't have time. I'm sure he would have enjoyed these activities as much as any teenager if he had had the chance to try them out.

*****

My father never even learned how to dance. Though many people think it strange for a person from Africa not to know how to dance, in my father's case, it makes sense. To this day, that man I proudly call Father doesn't know how to dance, and I personally have never seen him dance in public or at home. His friends like to tease him by inviting him to dance, but he simply ignores them.

One day, when I was fourteen, a traditional festival with a dance was organized in Agadji's central public area. Almost the entire population of about two hundred gathered. The atmosphere was so pleasant that everyone wanted to be part of it; everybody wanted to dance. The elderly people, adults, youths, and even little ones, including myself, were having great fun, Those too old to dance stood watching with their fragile bodies perched on their canes. In my village, we say these people are counting the days till they join our ancestors. Even those fragile elderly were beating the rhythm with their canes or fingers, which the music seemed to have miraculously healed of leprosy and arthritis. Even though their bodies did not allow them to physically dance, in their minds, they were in the middle of the crowd, dancing like never before.

My father was also at the party, but in spite of his youth and energy, he preferred to be a spectator. Many times he was invited to dance, and each time he refused. Finally, my mother snuck up behind my dad, grabbed his hand, and pulled him right into the middle of the happy throng. Because the whole village knew my dad had never danced before, everyone started screaming and applauding, as if to say, "Welcome to the party."

Because we knew my dad would do something to get away, my mom and us children were all watching very closely, laughing our hearts out. All of a sudden, my father made such a terrible face while grabbing his stomach that the crowd let my father go. As soon as he was released, sure enough, my dad walked proudly away and smiled with deep satisfaction, as if to say, "I told you so. I don't party. What kind of fool do you think I am? I got you."

It was very embarrassing for our family because here other men—fathers, husbands, or potential husbands—were showing off their talent in the traditional dances, but ours didn't—in fact, couldn't—dance and made fun of the celebration. Well, yes, it was embarrassing for us, but we were not surprised that our father would behave that way. Besides, it was a festival, and everybody was supposed to have fun, and without a doubt, my dad's episode added unexpected fun to the occasion. I think my dad enjoyed himself too. After all, didn't he make everybody applaud, laugh, and relax for a couple of minutes by faking a stomachache? That was by far the funniest thing I ever saw my dad do in public.

*****

Shortly after the funeral, my dad returned to his boss and explained how hard his life was about to become for him with his uncle and his support gone. He also told his boss about his decision to end the apprenticeship and return to Togo.

Then one evening, at the end of a hard day, my father was arranging tools in the tailor shop when he heard Mr. Emmanuel calling him into his living room. His first reaction was—*Oh my god! I hope my boss doesn't have any more assignments for me this evening. I'm really getting tired and I have to get up very early.*

Still, my father answered his boss right away and, within seconds, was standing next to him. My father almost passed out when Mr. Emmanuel invited him to have a seat.

This had never ever happened before. Normally, when the boss called, the apprentices always had to stand at attention, arms crossed, the way good soldiers respond to their superiors in the service. Why?

Simply to show respect. That's why my dad almost had a heart attack when Mr. Emmanuel invited him to sit down. At first, my dad thought he must have done something bad and was about to pay the price, but he really did not have time to analyze the situation because Mr. Emmanuel started speaking.

"Koffi," he said, "I'm sorry about your dear uncle Dete's death. Though I can't say I know how you feel at this particular moment, I can at least say that I understand all the hardships, especially financial, that you are experiencing. I had a talk with my uncle Ramfreed the other night about your situation, and we decided that, if you wish, you could move in and live with us as a servant. If you accept this proposal, then the day you graduate from your tailor training, you'll only have to bring me another two bottles of beer as ceremonial payment for your remaining tuition. What do you think?"

Though overwhelmed with great joy, my father did not hesitate and replied, "I will appreciate it very much, sir."

"Well," Mr. Emmanuel continued, "why not start moving in tomorrow? In fact, come with me now, and I'll show you your bedroom."

My father followed his boss without saying a word, saw his new living quarters, and then thanked both Mr. Emmanuel and Mr. Ramfreed before returning home that evening with a big smile on his young face. Truly, this deal brought hope to my father's future.

The next morning, my father moved into his boss' house. Of the fourteen apprentices, two other males, were living there as Mr. Emmanuel's servants. There were also two female servants working for Mrs. Florance Ramfreed, Emmanuel's uncle's wife. While the females were busy working for Mrs. Florance, my father and the other two males worked for their boss, Mr. Emmanuel. The male servants answered to Mr. Emmanuel before anybody else but were also made available to Mr. Ramfreed and his wife, Florance. It was the duty of my father and the male servants to wait on their boss during dinner before eating their own. The three shared a three-bedroom apartment known as the servants' quarter, which was next to their boss' living quarters.

Even though Mr. Emmanuel had developed special feelings for my dad after listening to his sad life story, he did not show or express these feelings to my father right away. In the beginning, he was as severe with my dad as he was with everyone else. He set traps to test my dad to see if he could catch him doing anything wrong, but my dad passed all tests.

My father often told us about these tests. Every morning, before my father went in to clean his boss' living quarters, including his private bedroom, Mr. Emmanuel would put coins in various places, mostly hidden under old, dirty clothes. His boss set this trap knowing full well my dad's situation as a poor orphan and in great need for money.

Every morning, my dad would go into his boss' living quarters and clean, and every morning, he would collect every coin he found and turn them in to his boss. My father vividly remembers this test mainly because it was one of the toughest he ever had to deal with.

One morning, Mr. Emmanuel once again called my dad to his living room, hugged him, and congratulated him for being such a loyal, honest servant. Then to the astonishment of my father, he promoted him to the position of head servant in the household, even though he was the newcomer. Because my dad's boss didn't have any children, he and his wife allowed my father to have access to their greatest secrets, keys, and special belongings.

My dad was asked to oversee the day-to-day operations of the household. His boss felt he deserved the position because of his honesty and good behavior. Still, this responsibility was a bit too much for my father. After all, he was the newest apprentice, a foreigner, and a teenager with no prior experience in overseeing others.

In addition, my dad was scared of his fellow servants' reactions—some were older and bigger than he was.

Luckily, his boss made it easy on him by backing him up, making sure everybody, older or younger, bigger or smaller, listened to my dad's orders.

This was especially important in an incident that broke out between my dad and an apprentice named Kwuassi. Unlike most apprentices, Kwuassi was from a middle-class family. His siblings were attending the most prestigious private schools in Hohoe. Kwuassi had ended up as a tailor apprentice because he was rebellious and, consequently, didn't do well in school. Kwuassi was about two years older than my father, and he was big and liked to intimidate people with his size.

One Friday evening, my dad asked Kwuassi to help the other apprentices clean up the tailor shop before going home. While the others were following my father's order, Kwuassi not only refused but also talked back to my father.

"Koffi," Kwuassi said to my dad, "you know what? I'm getting tired of taking stupid orders from you. This little cleaning job can be done without me. Plus, I think you and those sorry servants should be the ones to do these dirty little jobs, anyway. I don't have time to clean, not today, maybe tomorrow."

During the time he was addressing my father, Kwuassi did not know that Mr. Emmanuel happened to be overhearing. Kwuassi paused and then concluded his disrespectful speech. "Eh, Koffi, stop being so bossy, would you? After all, who do you think you are, you sorry foreigner?"

Kwuassi was about to walk out of the shop when Mr. Emmanuel's voice called out, "Kwuassi, big Kwuassi." He was so surprised that he almost wet his pants. His eyes got as big as an owl's.

"Kwuassi," Mr. Emmanuel said, as if he wasn't sure of what had been said, "come back. Did I just hear you talking to Koffi?"

There was total silence from Kwuassi.

"Come on," Mr. Emmanuel said, "answer my question. This is a better opportunity for you to talk back." He let his words sink in. "Let me remind you of something, Kwuassi. It is true that Koffi is a poor sorry foreigner, like you said, but he has a good head on his shoulders." Then his voice filled with rage. "Who are you? Maybe a proud Ghanaian with a sorry empty brain. You tell me—between the two of you, who weighs more?"

Big Kwuassi, too petrified to talk back, said nothing. "Sir Kwuassi," Mr. Emmanuel continued, making fun of him, "you are not going home this evening. You are grounded for three days, during which you'll have to take orders from Koffi and Koffi only. You go by my rules, or else I don't want to you see you back here as my apprentice. I'm going to notify your parents about your punishment."

After that day, no one has messed with my father, not even "Sir" Kwuassi.

Because of the special love, trust, and respect that Mr. Emmanuel had for him, his boss allowed my dad to take jobs outside the house on Saturdays and Sundays to save money for his graduation fees as well as have some pocket money. Every Saturday and Sunday, my dad worked on farms, mainly weeding cocoa and coffee. Because he made so little money, it took my father forever to save enough for his graduation. By the time he had saved the required amount, he had spent nine years with his boss instead of the expected four.

Rumors of my father's difficulties in Hohoe slowly reached his father's family in Agadji. Just a few weeks before my dad's graduation, his uncle Koumodji Edoh decided to send a trusted farmworker by the name of Moussa Pelelant as a special emissary. Moussa Pelelant arrived with a significant amount of money for my father for his graduation on March 14, 1949. As my father had already saved enough money for his graduation tuition, this additional money from his uncle Edoh came on handy for his expenses to move back to Togo.

After graduation, my father returned to Agadji, his native village, for a short stay. There he fell in love with an attractive young woman who, like himself, had just come back from a city in Ghana, Kedjebi, where she, too, had learned to be a tailor, only of women's clothes. The woman's name was Elizabeth Akoua, and she, too, was attracted.

Looking back, my parents always talk about how amazing it was that they were able to mutually fall in love and get married. In their village and society, most men claimed to have married the woman they loved, but the women did not necessarily feel the same way. In those days, women were almost always married to their husbands through the arranged marriage system; in fact, sometimes they were married against their will. Mutual love marriages either did not exist or were not very common.

A young girl could find herself a married woman overnight, often at the age of fifteen, if a secret deal had been made between the soon-to-be bride's and groom's families. The girl's family made the decision of who their daughter would marry, not herself. While my

Akposso tribe, like many others, valued marriages as a union between the bride and the groom, the bride's family had to look carefully at their soon-to-be new son. The final decision was based strongly on the social and economic background of the potential groom and his entire family's. The bride's family would have "big eyes" for men who were financially well off or whose family had a lot to offer the bride's family once the marriage had occurred. In those circumstances, the girl's opinion or feelings were completely irrelevant. What mattered were the dowry and other benefits the family could get.

My mother can be considered lucky that she fell for someone who at the same time had his eyes on her. My father and my mother quickly got married and moved to a city called Tomegbe, in the region of Wawa, on June 19, 1951. The city of Tomegbe is forty miles from Agadji near Togo's western border with Ghana. My dad decided to move there because he had relatives, including the Olympio, Edjimi, Agbetete, and Lokpo families, who cared about him and who were excited to have him start his business there.

In fact, Mr. Agbetete Kouakou had run into my father in Ghana toward the end of his apprenticeship and invited him to come to Tomegbe and open up his tailor shop.

In Tomegbe, my dad and his new bride were honorably received by their relatives. They were given a free one-bedroom apartment. My dad was also temporarily given free land to farm for a home garden if he or my mother wanted to have one, unlike with cash crops, where men or women can work in a small garden.

In Tomegbe, my dad opened up his first tailor shop, and then shortly after he was financially stable, my parents started their family.

In 1954, my parents had their first baby boy. After they had this first child, they modified their habit of sleeping in a totally dark room and started keeping the lantern on a small flame. Even though the lantern wasn't far from their bed, the room was still very dark: they could hardly see the lantern flame.

One night, the quiet of their room was destroyed. The baby suddenly started crying. He was crying so loudly that my parents knew he wasn't crying for food; they knew something was wrong with him.

Luckily, my father had developed the habit of sleeping with the flashlight close by for security reasons. His first reflex when he heard the baby's cry was to grab his flashlight. My dad jumped out of bed and started looking around for a visible enemy. He was determined to fight to protect his baby, his own blood.

My mother's reaction, like that of any mother who loves her children, was quick and decisive. She turned the light up so she could see and, with lightning speed, turned around and picked her baby up in her arms. She tried to breastfeed the baby, but it was clear he was not hungry; he was in such pain that he might have forgotten what his mom's breasts were for. It was then that my parents started worrying about the health of their first newborn.

In those days, small clinics, like the one in Tomegbe, were ill-staffed and were only open until 10:00 p.m. After that, either the clinics were closed until morning or perhaps there would be a poorly trained night nurse, who only knew how to take temperatures, do paperwork, and give vaccinations and injections. The good nurses, as there were never doctors in the clinics, would have already worked more than twenty hours and gone home too tired even to remember how to spell their own names correctly.

Knowing of these circumstances, my parents decided to wait to go to the clinic until the next morning. They stayed awake all night, hoping and praying that whatever was wrong with their baby would go away soon and that it would not be life-threatening.

My parents succeeded in keeping the baby stable throughout the night, even though he cried and threw up any food my mom tried to give him.

My parents, exhausted from staying up all night, were delighted to see first the dawn and then daylight finally come. Wasting no time, they went into action. My mother went straight to the clinic. My father stopped at his relatives to let them know the baby wasn't feeling good, and they were taking him to the clinic. Two of them got dressed and accompanied him.

By the time my father and his relatives arrived at the clinic, the "real" nurse had started examining the baby; his blood pressure and temperature had been taken, and he had received several shots. The nurse then told my parents that the baby was in fair condition and that he should be fine. The nurse asked my parents to bring the baby back to the clinic anytime. He also added that the baby's behavior of the night before had been a simple nightmare, nothing to worry about.

In fact, what the baby had experienced that night was worse than any nightmare, much worse. The baby had been inflicted with a typical African illness. Someone had come in the night, scared the baby, and taken something from him, something that neither shot nor blood pressure medicine could give back to him, namely his soul. Yes, his fragile soul had been stolen that night. My dad's enemies from his native village Agadji, including his dear uncle Edoh, had come and stolen his baby's soul away; that is why the baby wasn't feeling well. Still, my parents didn't know this; they were too naive to think of it as a possibility.

My parents returned home hoping that the magic touch of Western medicine would save their firstborn. My mother successfully breastfed her baby for the first time since the day before—more proof to my parents that the magic touch of the nurse was working.

Early in the afternoon, my parents were about to take a nap, not having slept the night before, when all of sudden the baby started crying and acting worse than before. My parents, who earlier had been showing signs of fatigue from their ordeal, got their energy back and again threw themselves into saving their baby's life. Everything happened very fast. Immediately, my parents returned to the clinic. This time, even though the same nurse tried everything he had learned in nursing school, nothing worked. The situation grew critical.

At four thirty that afternoon, an unwanted reality struck my parents—their beloved first child had passed away. The events from that moment till the baby was buried are too sad for my parents to recount.

According to my mother, the baby was killed by my father's relatives back in Agadji after my dad's dispute with them over a piece of land. My father claimed the land was his and that it had been unjustly taken from him while he was in Ghana.

Both my parents had good reasons to believe their baby had been mysteriously killed. First of all, the baby passed away just two days after my dad's return from Agadji and the argument. Secondly, their nine-day-old newborn had been healthy and not shown any sign of ill health until the night before his death. My dad was convinced his son had been killed "by voodoo curse" as punishment for daring to argue with his relatives and claiming his right to the land.

In a continent full of mysteries like Africa where the belief in and practice of voodoo is very strong, it's very common to see people one knows personally suffer from mysterious illnesses that lead to seriously sad consequences, such as mental illness or death, in a very short period of time. Modern medicine is of no help. The evidence for voodoo is so strong throughout that mysterious continent of mine that even my Christian faith has not been able to prevent me from acknowledging its presence.

*****

During the nineteenth century, when the Europeans came back to Africa four centuries after they had introduced slavery, it was with different intentions—intentions known in African history as the theory of the three C's—that is, to Civilize, Colonize, and Christianize the indigenous peoples.

During the slave trade, Europeans had faced for the most part either little or no opposition. In fact, sometimes local kings and chiefs had even cooperated with the Europeans and enjoyed selling their prisoners of war and later their own people to the slave buyers.

Unlike that first contact, the second contact with indigenous Africans was marked by resistance throughout the entire continent of Africa. Some of the bloodiest resistance happened in Southern Africa under the reign of great kings named Kinsuwayo and Tchaka Zulu. In Western Africa, we, too, had our heroes: King Gbehanzin of Dahomey, the present-day Republic of Benin; King Ossei Tutu of the Gold Coast, the now Republic of Ghana; and King Samory Toure of the Republic of Mali, to name a few.

Unfortunately, all these resistances were put down due to the superiority of the weapons of the Europeans who used powder guns against the bow and arrows of the indigenous warriors. Another reason for the defeat of the Africans was a general physical weakness of the population. After several centuries of slave trade, the continent had been stripped of its strongest people, people who, under normal circumstances, could have put up a better fight against the Europeans.

It was not until after those main oppositions were put to violent ends that the European invaders started dividing the continent of Africa into small pieces of land for their occupation. Though Africa today seems to have been primarily divided between two European countries, France and Great Britain, other European countries were involved as well, such as Germany, Spain, Portugal, Italy, and Belgium. In fact, the idea of territorial expansion in Africa began with King Leopold II of Belgium who in the 1800s sent an explorer by the name of Savorgna de Brazza to explore the Congo River in Central Africa. Almost at the same time, another explorer, actually a journalist, by the name of Stanley was sent to the same region by a British news agency, *The Daily Graft*, to write an article about the Congo River. It was the river rivalry between these two explorers and their sponsors that opened the awareness of European countries to the possibilities of the African continent—a place where plantations of cotton, coffee, and cocoa could be raised, from where minerals, lumber and rubber could flow to Europe to support their growing industrial revolution, and to where the Europeans could sell their manufactured goods.

The European colonizers heavily invested in the infrastructure of their new colonies by building roads, railroads, seaports, and later airports to facilitate the shipment of raw materials to their European destinations. They also invested in the well-being of the indigenous people through introducing modern Western medicine, especially vaccines, that effectively fought illnesses, such as leprosy, malaria, tuberculosis, cholera, and yellow fever that were out of control in Africa.

Another major area in which the European colonizers invested in was the expansion of their Christian faith. Throughout the colonies, churches were being built alongside roads.

The course of events as they occurred in all of Africa could be followed in my own country of Togo in West Africa.

In the summer of 1884, the very first European colonizers' ship led by a German named Natchingal landed on the shore of a tiny fishing village called Agbodrafo, located on the Atlantic Ocean, half-way between the former capital city of Aneho and the present-day capital city of Lome. From Agbodrafo, the German colonizers moved for strategic reasons to the other side of a lagoon, known today as Lake Togo, to the North of Agbodrafo village. At this strategic location, called by the natives Togodo, which in Ewe, a language spoken in the area, means "to the water's edge," the Germans first signed a treaty of protectorate with the local Ewe tribe's King Mlapa III on July 5, 1884. From here, the Germans would expand their occupation into the mainland of the country and later into other parts of West Africa. Togodo eventually became the first capital city of this German colony. This first German settlement of Togodo would give birth to the country of Togo.

The Germans spent a lot of time developing the economy of their colony, Togo. Railroad tracks, seaports, airports, roads (though mostly dirt), big government buildings, including impressive governor's residences, were built to last under the careful supervision of the tough, hardworking Germans. Almost a hundred years later, some of the structures still exist and are used today.

Vast plantations of coconut trees were developed throughout southern Togo, mostly along the coast. While teak plantations were established through the country, coffee and cocoa, the two most lucrative export crops of Togo, were concentrated in the southwestern part of the country.

During their relatively short reign in Togo as colonizers, the Germans gained the admiration of the Togolese for being hard workers, an admiration many Togolese still hold. The Germans were equally proud of the work they had done with Togo economically and named it a muster colony, meaning "model colony."

In Kamina, a small village located about forty miles north of Lome, the current capital of Togo, the Germans built the most powerful communication post in all of Sub-Saharan Africa of that era.

The Kamina communication post was designed to facilitate communication between German ships in the Atlantic Ocean; it was so powerful that it soon attracted the envy of and induced discomfort in English and French colonizers in the region. In fact, during World War II, when the German forces were seriously weakened in Europe and unable to militarily defend their colonies around the world, Togo, then Togoland, became an easy target for the joint French and English military forces, and the communication post of Kamina became the very first target. After two months of heavy fighting, the post was destroyed, but because it had been so well built, its ruins remain to this day, making the village of Kamina a very popular colonial period site visited by tourists in Togo.

Following the defeat of the Germans, Togoland was divided between the French and the English and disappeared from the map. The French already controlled land to the east, which today is the Republic of Benin; they simply attached their portion of Togoland to their colony. To the West, the English controlled the area then known as the Gold Coast (today's Republic of Ghana); they attached their portion to their colony.

The tiny country of Togo that exists on the map today is less than half the size of the original German Togoland. It is made up of the part that the French forces who moved in from Dahomey occupied during the war against the Germans.

The rest of the original German Togoland, which was occupied by the British forces during the war and known to the Togolese as Togo Britanique or Britain-Togo and known to the international community as the Volta Region, is still part the Republic of Ghana—the most fertile and the richest part. In the eyes of the Togolese, the Volta Region represents a bitter reminder of scars left by the great world wars.

For many years, after Togo was placed under the supervision of France by the League of Nations, the French did not devote any effort into building or expanding the economy aspects of Togo, partly because the French had inherited the work done by the Germans; instead, the French devoted much effort to Christianizing the native people.

Many French, mostly Catholic missionaries, were sent to Togo. Catholic churches and cathedrals were built, along with schools, throughout the country, including in the northern part of the country, which for years had been essentially neglected. In fact, some of the most influential schoolteachers in local communities were French priests or missionaries. Seminaries were also built, and more and more native people were encouraged to abandon their traditional beliefs and connections to their departed ancestors and instead go to church as many times a week as possible as well as to enter the priesthood, which was considered the ultimate sacrifice to our Creator a man could make; it was also the most likely way to get to heaven after death.

In my Plateaux region and in my own Agadji village, events followed the same course during the French era.

I still remember that day as a little boy when I got tired of listening to people talking about Pere or Father Cotez and finally asked my parents who Father Cotez was. Father Cotez had been the very first Catholic—missionary or priest—to come to my village. He had been the one who laid the foundation for the spread of the Catholic religion in my village; he had also laid the foundation of the St. Augustine Church that still stands tall and beautiful as ever in my village. Father Cotez was eventually transferred to Tomegbe in the county of Wawa, where my father had first worked as a tailor and where I was born. Father Cotez had been very popular in my Agadji as he was throughout the entire Catholic community in the Plateaux Region, but he was even more so in Tomegbe where he lived out his life, died, and was buried at the age of ninety-five or so.

Shortly after Father Cotez was transferred to Tomegbe, Father Jean Paul Felder arrived in the early '60s. Father Jean Paul was never assigned to any other village. Upon his arrival in Agadji, Father Jean Paul Felder inherited a well-established parish where the Roman Catholic faith was growing very fast. In Agadji, the center of the parish of St. Augustine, he inherited the beautiful St. Augustinian Church and a Western-style four-bedroom house, which for the longest time was the best house in the village. It was the only home until recently that had a generator for electricity and modern toilets. The priest's compound or "mission" is located west of the village, sur-rounded by mostly oranges, guavas, and tall teak trees. Perhaps these inheritances were among the reasons why he may have left Agadji on only very rare occasions for a day or two to celebrate mass in the surrounding villages, but he always came back.

The main mission assigned to Father Jean Paul Felder was to develop and encourage the expansion of the Catholic faith in the parish, and Father Jean Paul did his job. One very important way of involving people in the Catholic faith was through education. Under Father Jean Paul's supervision, classrooms were added to the Catholic school, which was located right in front of his residence. More and better-qualified teachers were hired. Strict discipline, including the spanking of lazy or undisciplined students, was encouraged. At the same time, well-behaved and hardworking students were rewarded by Father Jean Paul personally; he would present them with note-books, pens, schoolbooks, and pencils at the end of each school year just before recess. All students ended the year with a souvenir, and group pictures were taken—each grade with their teachers and, of course, with Father Jean Paul.

Father Jean Paul also built a bookstore called Librairie bon Pasteur near his residence. He hired fulltime employees and trained them himself, and whenever he could find time, he worked alongside them. At the beginning of each school year, he would work there full-time, for the library was always packed from opening to closing.

In the social arena, Father Jean Paul and others promoted sports and culture groups. Soccer games were encouraged, and a tennis court was built on the mission compound. Also, on the compound, Father Jean Paul built a European-style building known as the Culture Center, where movies were shown and plays were performed.

The most unforgettable social activity established during Father Jean Paul Felder's era, which affected the entire Plateaux Region and brings "good old time" memories to villagers of all ages, was the Christian youth group known as CV AV. The group has performed a wide variety of plays since its beginning, including Bible stories such as the nativity and plays about everyday life; everyone still enjoys watching them. The CV AV group, led by one of the most energetic schoolteachers of that time, Mr. Akpossogna Martin, occasionally performed in the surrounding villages as well.

The priests also helped to bring modern conveniences to our village. Father Jean Paul bought a large power generator that provided electricity on the main streets of both my village, Agadji, and the neighboring village of Amlame.

Later, another priest, sent by the same Roman Catholic congregation in France to assist Father Jean Paul, helped develop a water system that provided both villages with a public system of clean running water; this priest, called Younger or Second Father by the villagers, was named Father Cochere.

In the area of religion, the actions of Fathers Jean Paul, Cochere, and later Matiss were even more remarkable. Under their supervision, two huge, one-story modern buildings were built in Agadji, four miles from their compound. To this day, the buildings remain the compound run by European nuns that have helped the priests spread the Christian faith among the native women. The nuns also have helped recruit and train all nuns (mostly women native to Africa) who have wished to serve in Togo.

When I was growing up, the educational program at my village Catholic school was a combination of the courses taught in public schools, along with mandatory religion courses.

I remember during my early school years when the entire school compound would go to church for an early morning prayer session known as Students' Mass on Tuesdays prior to classes. In addition, every morning, before the Togolese national flag was raised, before the national anthem "The Land of Our Ancestors" was sung, and before any school announcements were made, all the students of all the grades assembled in front of their classrooms and recited in one voice one Our Father and three Hail Mary, under the watchful eyes of the priests and schoolteachers.

In addition to taking religion classes, male students were encouraged to continue their education in the seminaries and consider entering the priesthood; likewise, female students were encouraged to become nuns. I never made it to a seminary; nevertheless, I came very close to being in one when I served the priests as one of the few altar boys from the village.

The Catholic priests in Agadji were largely successful in converting the entire village of Agadji to and maintaining them in the Roman Catholic faith. In many ways, these missionaries were successful in getting the natives to adore the statues of Catholic saints instead of their traditional mud representations of the souls of their ancestors.

As a seven-year-old, I remember being aware of a little hut next to a tall mango tree behind our kitchen. The hut belonged to our neighbor, Mr. Koffi Edjignon. Then one day, the hut was gone. As a child, I had never questioned my parents about the meaning of the small house nor had I played close to it; it was off limits to my siblings and myself. Later, as an adult, when I finally asked my parents where had the little hut gone, they told me that Father Jean Paul had ordered its destruction because he didn't like it. As it turned out, that little hut had contained a mud representation of Mr. Koffi's family ancestors, where he would occasionally pour some palm wine or red cooking oil and sometimes sacrifice chickens as a way of communicating with his ancestors. Through these ancestors, Mr. Koffi would ask our Creator for whatever he needed, such as good crops or health. Unfortunately, this traditional way of praying, called giving libation, was unwelcomed by the Catholic religion.

One morning, Father Jean Paul Felder had gone to Mr. Koffi's house and convinced him to destroy *that* mud house himself; Mr. Koffi did destroy it but with great hesitation. After the destruction of the hut, the same Mr. Koffi joined the Roman Catholic Church in the village. He even became a top church committee member and was in charge of keeping children quiet during mass, especially on Sundays. I remember how scared we children were of Mr. Koffi because with Father Jean Paul's blessing, he gave quick attention to any troublesome child during Mass. As a matter of fact, we gave him the nickname of Mr. Kokoliko, meaning "he who knocks on people's heads."

What happened in my tiny village during colonization and Christianization happened to all of Togoland as well as to the entire continent of Africa. Though the Europeans have the right to claim victory in some areas of their endeavors, to this day, a vast majority of Africans still struggle with the decision to fully abandon their traditional religious practices, including the giving of libations and the sacrificing of animals such as chicken, goats, and sheep. In many ways, these traditional beliefs make Africans who they are, and many believe that in giving up the traditional practices, they will lose their own identity and it will be replaced by a Western Christian faith that has been forced upon them by outsiders.

Clearly, Europeans have failed in their efforts to change their colonized African natives into 100 percent devoted Christians. One reason for this failure lies in an inconsistency in the teachings of the Roman Catholic faith on one hand and practice on the other. Africans, for instance, have realized that even though Europeans declared animist practices of sacrificing animals and of having "graven images" to be barbaric, Christianity has had both. In the Old Testament, references to the killing of animals for God was common. Abraham was even asked by God to sacrifice his only son, Isaac. Africans found it strange that while Europeans asked them to abandon their man-made representations of ancestors, Catholic churches are full of statues representing influential saints and on top, in front, and inside of every European-style Catholic church, there is the sign of the cross.

Another reason conservative animists in Africa have rejected Christianity is that they view it as a religion of repressive colonizers and former slave runners and owners. Islam, practiced mostly in Northern Africa, is viewed similarly.

Those Africans who have become Christians live today with the constant dilemma that being 100 percent Christian requires them to ignore the historical beliefs of their own history, and perhaps even of their very own existence. The vast majority of Africans find peace for their souls by finding some way to combine Christianity with traditional beliefs. These beliefs make it very difficult for an African to be a strict Christian because, as it is said, Africa has its mysteries. These mysteries may be a natural part of Africa or they may have been created by animist worshipers and their priests who have tremendous supernatural powers or perhaps the mysteries originated in both sources.

Before the Europeans landed on the African continent with their plans to Colonize, Civilize, and Christianize, there was already strong belief among the natives that "Africa has its mysteries"; this belief refers to the supernatural forces in which most Africans believe. Africans, for instance, believe in the continued existence of the soul after death much as Christians believe in life after death. The difference is that unlike Christians, Africans fear their dead, worship them, or use them as intermediaries to reach the God they believe lives above, underneath, or around us (God's exact place of residence depends on the beliefs of a specific people.) For Africans, a family member who dies becomes physically nonexistent but spiritually exists forever and, as a spirit, is closer to God the Creator. This strong belief has convinced Africans that the best way to have their prayers answered by God the Creator is to send them "in care of" their dead relatives who are closer to God. To accomplish this, traditional prayers and rituals are used; these later became known to the Western world as animism or is sometimes called voodoo.

Animism involves sacrificing animals, mainly chicken, goats, or sheep, during traditional ceremonies. Sacrifices are made to ask for or give thanks to God for such things as rain, better crops, the birth of a child, or an abundance of food. During these ceremonies, dead relatives are asked to play the role of intermediaries to God, much as Catholics appeal to saints in the Roman Catholic faith. Most often, sacrifices are done in special locations where the dead are represented by statues made of stones or mud, although sacrifices can be done anywhere because souls are everywhere.

As I said, the dead are not worshiped as gods; instead, they are used to reach the Supreme Creator of earth and heaven. Animists understand very well that there is a God.

The biggest concern is how to reach God since it's clear no living being can see him. Animists conclude that since God is like soul and since after death one becomes a soul, the way to reach God is through ancestors and recent relatives who once lived among them. Because the dead have shared in the experiences of the living and now are closer to Him, they can serve as "ambassadors" to God.

In the animist community in Africa, the souls of the elderly, especially men, are very precious, even sacred. The older a person, the more mature the soul and the better the ancestor will know how to negotiate with God on behalf of the living. Depending on the size of the family, women, ancestors, who lived to be very old, may occasionally be mentioned, called forth, or invoked. However, most women and all those who die young are not usually invoked because of a belief in the weak nature of females and in the immaturity of youth.

In Africa, especially West Africa, voodoo is a reality. Animist priests have supernatural powers that can kill, harm, or heal. While in the West arguments are generally solved by lawsuits or at gunpoint, in Africa, voodoo is often used to harm or kill one's enemy.

If one wants to harm someone, all the person has to do is pay an animist priest who will use his supernatural powers to put a curse on the intended victim. In a matter of hours or days, the voodoo will start to affect the victim. Depending on the nature of the curse, the victim may have an accident, go blind, divorce his/her partner, be forced into exile, or die. In 99 percent of the cases, the curse has the planned effect. The only time the curse may not work is when the intended victim receives protection from another voodoo priest.

I know a young man in Agadji who mysteriously left his family in the '70s and never returned. This man was my uncle on my father's side. I remember when I was a child, this young man would cut the hair of my brother Fidel, my dad, and myself at least once a month. He was also one of the best soccer players in my region.

One morning, this uncle left his wife and his three boys and one girl, aged ten years to three months, for an unknown destination and never returned. Rumor says his older brother, Mr. L, went to see an animist priest who chased him into exile so that Mr. L could have their family lands and farms all to himself. Nobody knows if the rumors are true, but the sad fact is that my uncle has been gone so long that people are starting to forget him. His whereabouts are an unsolved mystery.

However, like I said, not all the voodoo priests are bad. While some use their power to do harm, others use their powers to protect people or cure illnesses.

Ms. Gladice, one of my favorite cousins from my dad's side, in Amlame village is still alive today because her relatives, including my father, searched until they finally found the right medicine man to cure her from a mysterious illness that she had suffered from for more than a decade.

The entire Adade family considers Ms. Gladice one of our favorite relatives for strong reasons. She was the daughter of my father's late sister, Adjuwa, to whom my father owes all respect, gratitude, and honor; Adjuwa to whom my family owes its very existence today, for she was the one who took good care of our father after their mother's death in Amlame.

Ms. Gladice, I still remember, used to hand down to our older sister, Pauline, her clothes and shoes that no longer fit; she did this every time we visited her in Amlame. Pauline must be fifteen, Fidel twelve, myself ten, and our younger sister, Jeanne, eight.

Ms. Gladice once lived a good life. Being one of the most beautiful girls in her village, an ideal representation of an African "queen," a perfect candidate for the title of "Miss Togo," Ms. Gladice enjoyed dating nice-looking, wealthy men and lived a comfortable life.

A few years after the birth of her only child, Bebe, who, like her mother Gladice, is very attractive, cousin Gladice started suffering from mysterious illnesses—one day a headache, the next chest pains, swelling of arms and legs the next, and so forth. For more than five years, my dear cousin Gladice knocked at the doors of every single medical center and hospital in the country in search of a solution to her health problem; unfortunately, her situation seemed only to get worse.

It was then that my father and her relatives in Amlame decided to turn to traditional medicine. By that time, Ms. Gladice had become so weak that she could barely perform any physical activity by herself. For more than seven years, during which my dear cousin Gladice became something close to a vegetable, more than twenty traditional medicine men tried to alleviate her suffering. These traditional medicine men either failed or only managed to alleviate her pain temporarily. Her life became a pure living hell. It became clear to everyone that Gladice was eventually going to die with her misery.

It was with that sad conviction that I myself left my country, Togo, for the United States the afternoon of June 12, 1989. Then in the summer of 1992, my brother Fidel told me a happy story about our cousin Gladice. Thanks to help from myself, the Togolese government, Richard Rosenberg, and my forever friend, Su Cutler, Fidel was in Kalamazoo attending a six-month agricultural training program at Tillers International.

"Peter," as Fidel, my mom, and older sister Pauline liked to call me, "you are not going to believe this!"

"What is it?" I asked.

Without any hesitation, Fidel continued, "Some powerful *bokono* (traditional) medicine man successfully cured our cousin Gladice of her illness."

"*Edjunu*," I replied, meaning "You're lying" in my native language Akposso.

"No, I'm not," Fidel said and then he continued as if to reassure me. "It only took this *bokono* from some remote village up on the mountain less than a week to clean cousin Gladice's body of all those illnesses that have almost killed her. As I speak, cousin Gladice can walk, do anything inconceivable only a few months ago."

I almost fainted upon hearing that story about our dear cousin Gladice. Shortly after Fidel went back home to Togo, he sent me a picture of Gladice taken in Agadji during one of her visits to my family. Her recovery is hard to believe, but it is true. African medicine men do possess healing power as well as the power to harm.

As I said, it's hard—very hard, indeed—for an African to ignore the realities and the mysteries of Africa.

*****

My father had a direct encounter with the mysteries of Africa. Shortly after the death of his and my mother's firstborn son, they asked an animist priest what had caused the death. They were not surprised when the priest told them the baby had been killed by my father's family to punish him for arguing over some family land. My father recalls that the argument took place during his previous visit to Agadji. He had left my mother behind in Tomegbe.

On the third day after his arrival in Agadji, he was called to the head of the family's home where other family members were already waiting. The family was gathered to render a decision in an argument between my father and a cousin as to who had the right to keep a piece of land located just outside the village.

The family meeting was actually quite short because a decision had really been reached the day before the meeting. As my father had inherited the land from the uncle he had cared for in the hospital in Kpalime until his uncle died there, the senior family members announced that my father should keep the land. As expected, my father's cousin was not pleased with the seniors' decision and threatened my father, saying angrily, "Koffi! You better let go of that piece of land, or you will regret it for the rest of your life."

My father, ever the diplomat, shot back, "Go to hell! This land has always been mine. Besides, you have more lands than you can farm. I really don't understand what your problem is. Maybe you are so greedy that you want to own the entire family's lands. Let me tell you, the family will not allow that to happen."

My father never took his cousin's threat seriously until he returned to Tomegbe a few days later, and only then when his first-born child died mysteriously.

To this day, my mother has never forgiven my dad for making the mistake of arguing with his relative—a mistake that resulted in the death of her firstborn. Likewise, she will never forgive my dad's family for, as she puts it, "killing my baby, my first son."

Even though my dad has always been a devout Catholic, after the death of his son, while he kept his Catholicism, he began to consult regularly with the animist priest who had revealed the cause of his son's death. The purpose of these consultations was to obtain protection for his family—at that time composed only of my mother and himself.

The reasons people see animist priests may seem similar to those that motivate us to see modern medical doctors, but they are actually more complex. An animist priest, unlike a medical doctor, deals with physical and mystical problems. A typical consultation with an animist priest involves going to his or her home and explaining one's problem. The priest carefully listens and then tries to solve the problem. For instance, if one has a child who is having nightmares and who cries every night, the priest will consult with his or her person supernatural forces through rituals to determine the source of the child's problem. If the child is being hunted by a jealous neighbor or relative, the priest will find out. Once the source of the problem has been found, the priest, like a medical doctor, will describe the remedy and the cost one must follow to solve the problem.

Depending on the problem, in most cases, the priest will ask for money and animals, such as chicken, ducks, goats, or sheep. The priests will usually request that the animals be of a specific color. All white or all black are the most often requested, depending on the situation and on the priest. While some of the animals are scarified to help solve the problem, the priests make sure to keep something for themselves as partial payment for their services. Then depending on the priest and the solution, some of the sacrificed animals are cooked and served by the priest to the clients before they leave. These ceremonially prepared dishes taste very different from everyday food because of the unusual spices and medicinal herbs used. In addition to the different tastes, these meals are prepared without salt and pepper. Many people eat these meals with a sorry expression on their faces, but they dare not protest.

*****

Not long after the death of their first child, my mom was pregnant again; this time in 1956 they had a baby girl whom they named Pauline. A couple of months after Pauline's birth, my dad made another major mistake related to his two religions. He ended his relationship with the animist priest who had been protecting the family since the death of his first child. My dad terminated the relationship so that he could again fully devote himself to his Catholic faith. The result was another painful experience.

During the time that my father was not consulting the animist priest and had put his connections there on the back burner, my mother became pregnant and gave birth to another baby girl. While Pauline had lived, thanks to the priest's protection, the second baby girl wasn't so lucky. She died within two weeks after being born. The reason for her death is still unknown. My parents could think of only two reasons: either my dad's family members were still mad at him and had struck again, or the animist priest himself was not happy that my dad had stopped paying for protection and had taken revenge on my father by killing his second baby daughter.

Because of their doubts about the cause of this second death, my mom, while avoiding directly accusing my father or his family, advised my father to reconsider and to again seek "un-Catholic" protection for the family. My dad himself was extremely upset by these events, and he vowed that from now on, while he would keep his Catholic religion, he would also maintain his African traditions. He made the decision to use any power available to protect his family and remain loyal to the "animist" faith as well as to the Catholic faith.

*****

Despite the success of Western medicine, the truth is, there are still medical problems in Africa and mysterious illnesses that it cannot cure. However, these mysterious illnesses can be cured in a brief amount of time by a traditional African medicine man.

In my own tribe, there are mysterious weapons called Tsakatu or Agotu, which are used to hurt or kill people as far away as one thousand miles. Tsakatu or Agotu are not physical weapons; they are simple incantations or curses used by animist priests or others who have the power.

Let me try to explain how Agotu and Tsakatu work. After combining power and words, the "magician" selects an object to be used as a "bullet" to carry the curse into the body of the victim. Objects frequently used in my tribe are small stones, dry corn seeds, fish hooks, and the like. Once the object has been selected, the animist priest sends it to the victim through magic forces by pronouncing the name and location of the victim and stating the time the curse is to begin affecting the victim. Usually, within an hour, the victim will indeed start experiencing severe pains. Depending on the part of the body the cursed objects are sent into (head, stomach, heart, back, legs, or arms), the victim might die in minutes, hours, or days.

Agotu is by far the more dangerous of the two. There are few medicine men who can find a cure for Agotu, and it kills faster than Tsakatu within hours of being performed. The easiest way to explain the main difference between Agotu and Tsakatu is that while both curses are designed to harm their victims, Tsakatu takes longer to kill its victim, while Agotu can kill almost instantly.

Tsakatu is considered less dangerous not only because it takes a longer time to kill someone but because it is easier to find someone with the power to cure it. It is said that few medicine men have the guts to go through the mystical rituals that it takes to possess the power to counteract Agotu.

Modern medicine is powerless against both. It cannot even identify the problem, let alone try to find a cure. Not even the most powerful microscope or X-ray can identify the strange cursed objects sent into the body of a Tsakatu or Agotu victim. Only traditional medicine doctors—voodoo priests, if you will—have the power to deal with these illnesses.

Nowhere in Togo are Agotu or Tsakatu victims sent to a hospital. Families who have made the mistake of sending a loved one who has been cursed with Tsakatu or Agotu to a hospital have regretted the action, often losing their loved one.

I remember the death of an uncle on my mother's side.

He was in his early forties, a college teacher in the neighboring country of Ivory Coast. He became sick with a mysterious illness, and his friends took him to a hospital in Abidjan, the capital city. Two days later, he lost his sight, his ability to speak, and his mind, and it was not Alzheimer's; Alzheimer's does not strike that fast. Frightened by his rapid deterioration, the doctors and his friends finally flew him home to Togo where his mother lived. By the time he arrived in Togo, it was too late to save his life. He died two days later, two days after my departure to study in the United States of

America. Rumor said one of his friends in the Ivory Coast had put a voodoo curse, something like Agotu, on him. This friend supposedly thought my uncle was having an affair with his wife. My uncle's life might have been saved had his friends known a medicine man with the power to clear my uncle's body of the voodoo curse, but as the Ivory Coast was a foreign country with different traditions, it was not possible for them to find the right and immediate answer to my uncle's illness.

Years ago, all "sick" people were sent to the hospital; unfortunately, by the time modern doctors realized that the health problem of a patient exceeded their knowledge and sent them to a traditional doctor, it was too late. Today some African countries, including Togo, are making room in their hospital for traditional practices—much the way acupuncture treatment is associated with modern medicine in China and elsewhere. The purpose is to improve the health care system by treating all health problems in one place.

The era of denying the effectiveness of traditional African medicine is finally coming to an end.

*****

Africa, indeed, has its mysteries that even Africa herself may not understand, but we have learned they must be dealt with in African ways. My father should have known better than to ignore the mysteries of his motherland, Africa.

*****

After the loss of a second child, my father was unable to be impartial in his judgment; his grief prevented him from being open-minded or moderate. He decided once more to respect his African traditions while trying to remain a "good" Christian. He was dead serious that he would do anything to protect his family of three: himself, his wife, and Pauline. This decision was one of the toughest he had to face early in his married life. My father would have preferred either to stick 100 percent with his African traditions or be

100 percent Catholic, but like many other African, my father was not completely at peace with following only one.

He couldn't live a 100 percent Christian life in the middle of Africa's mysteries and realities, so my father became a "moderate" Christian—a solution many Africans adopt. He, of course, realized that trying to stick to both his African traditions and his Catholic faith would be hard. He would not be considered a "good" African, and therefore, he would be a traitor to his own traditions. Neither would he be thought a "good" Christian. Still, he did what he felt he had to do to help his family.

The pain his decision caused him is similar to that of a child born of an interracial relationship in the United States. This child is not 100 percent white or black. The sad fact is that this child is often rejected by and not fully integrated into either the black or white community.

To this day, my father is serious about his Catholic faith. He goes to church every Sunday like many Christians. He attends to morning and evening prayers the way a "good Christian" will. He reads his Bible whenever he has the chance, especially in the evening and on Sunday afternoons. He even practices his Latin at home in his free time.

My father, like many of the people in my village, has the European missionaries to thank for their ability to read. The missionaries' work has been very impressive. Even though the illiteracy rate is still high, missionaries have successfully taught average people how to read their Bible that the missionaries often translated into the people's native language. They also taught our people to sing and pray in European languages, such as French and Latin. As you may know, Latin plays an important role in Roman Catholicism; therefore, it was very important that one knew how to say at least one prayer or to sing at least one song in Latin.

For instance, in my country, no matter what native language is being used to celebrate the Mass, there has to be at least one prayer or song in Latin. Every single inhabitant of my village knows at least one Latin Catholic song, the credo. I was told that the reason the credo has to be in Latin is so that a Catholic from any part of the world attending a Roman Catholic church anywhere can participate in mass, even in a place with a language he/she can't speak. In other words, the credo and other Latin verses in the Roman Catholic Church serve as a bridge between all worshipers. I can image how wonderful my illiterate parents would feel in Italy, for example, where they could not even say, "*Buon giorno*," meaning "Good morning," but they could sing along with the credo in Latin with Italians at church.

Having been taught the importance of Latin in bringing Catholics together, I myself was surprised and disappointed when I went to St. Augustine Catholic Church in Kalamazoo, Michigan. Here, the credo is not sung in Latin. Everything is in English and nothing is in Latin. I have often wondered why, if Latin is supposed to be the root of the Roman Catholic faith, do US churches not use it? Does it represent a break from Roman Catholic principles in the United States? Is it a sign of deep love for the English language? Is this a result of a simple desire to change the status quo, by Americanizing the Catholic Church the way Americans Americanize everything? Or is it a sign of laziness in learning a foreign language?

I remember being surprised and impressed by my father's ability to sing and pray in Latin. I enjoyed going to church just to listen to him pray and to hear him sing.

My dad is not the type that sings often at home; in fact, his singing is as rare as a dog's tears. Even though my father does not sing as much as mother, he has a very beautiful, serious voice. Since he had such a gift, I wondered why my father did not sing in the church choir like my mother and other family members. so I asked him one day, "Son," he replied, "I would love to but I just don't have the time." His excuse sounded somewhat flimsy until I counted up the amount of time required for choir practices, which were held evening from eight to ten thirty—more than ten hours per week.

Despite not being in the choir, my dad holds the rules of the Catholic Church in high regard. He goes to confession, pays his yearly tithe to the church, and takes part in church activities. My father enjoys being involved in his church, his community, and, above all, his Christian faith.

*****

Still, my father also pays attention to his African heritage, values, and traditions. Clearly, my dad's dilemma now, as well as back then, was how to be a good Christian and a good African. Anytime something goes wrong in his family, especially if there is an illness, my dad kneels and prays. Then depending on the nature of the problem, he is as quick to seek the solution inside his African traditions as he is to consult modern medicine; he makes his choice based on whichever he feels will help the most at the time, given the circumstances.

Two French proverbs give insight into my father's lifestyle. The first states: "Mordu une fois, prudence une autre," meaning "We always learn from our mistakes." Critics might accuse my father of failing to be a strong Christian. Perhaps this is true; at the same time, his behavior is understandable, I think. He shouldn't be blamed for his double lifestyle. My father was unable to live only a Christian life because of the realities confronting him, especially the deaths of two children.

The second French proverb says: "L'homme nait bon, mais la nature le corrompt," meaning "We were all born to be good but are corrupted by our environment." In other words, whether we are wealthy or poor, thief or honest, we are the product of our environment. Hence, it is more likely for a nice family to raise nice, decent children; by the same token, it's more likely for a family of thieves to breed thieves. It is more likely for a family living on the streets, for instance, or on welfare to breed children who live the same life. Why? Because children often don't know any better or differently than what their parents do. Or as they say, like father like son or like mother like daughter or monkeys see monkeys do. While I agree that there are situations where children raised by bad parents have turned out well and vice versa, I believe that something must have happened to have changed that individual's behavior from good to bad or vice versa. In addition to the family, society can have a strong influence through gangs, church organizations, social programs, and role models.

As for my father, had he had a choice, he would have preferred to live a quieter, simpler life. He would have either stuck to his African traditions or been a plain Christian. However, his life, like that of many other Africans, was the result of the meeting of the Christianity of the European colonizers with the animism of Africa. My father, like millions of Africans living lives with a double religion, are the products of their environment.

*****

My parents were in Agadji during a family visit when a third living child, a baby boy, was born; this child is my older brother Fidel. The baby brought joy to the family, especially to my dad, and a deep satisfaction to my mom. After the death of her first son, my mother had been frightened of not having another boy—a situation that in Africa often leads to divorce or leads to the husband taking a second, third, or fourth wife. Clearly, the birth of this male child may have secured my mom's marriage; in any case, she was relieved.

In my tribe, having a son for the husband is a must. A son is everything; no matter what the son is like, he is the heir of the family. A son is the symbol of the family tree; he carries on the family name. A daughter is also welcomed in a typical African family, but the son gets most of the attention and the best schooling. He clearly receives preferential treatment over his female siblings. The general belief is that while the son carries on the family name and keeps the family's wealth in place, the daughter gets married and leaves her dad's home, trading her last name for her husband's.

In our family, my dad's favorite child has always been Pauline, our eldest sister; still, he loves his first son, Fidel, and respects him more than anyone else in the family because Fidel is the carrier of the family name, plain and simple.

Africans love their sons, there is no doubt about that, but they prefer a well-balanced family, made up of sons and daughters, as each sex plays a special role in the family.

As a result, my dad was additionally thrilled with Fidel's birth because now his family was nicely balanced. Father looked on Fidel as filling the role of his companion; my mom had Pauline. No matter how close Pauline became with her dad, she was after all female and, therefore, would do more with her mother than with her father.

Likewise, even if son Fidel became close to his mother, Fidel would still have to deal with his father more because they would be forced by society's rules to spend more time together and get along. Terrified by the thought of losing another son, my father decided to show the whole world that he was indeed a changed man, a true African, since the death of his second child. Right after Fidel's birth in 1960, my father took him to an animist priest to have traditional protective ceremonies performed. The result can be seen today on Fidel; he has three scars on each side of his face, next to his ears.

Those scars were to protect baby Fidel from evil forces, especially those sent by the family's enemies, who might make a third attempt for revenge on the family by taking his life. At the end of the ceremony, Fidel was given a traditional name, Kable, meaning in my language "a baby boy born after a previous child who has died."

My dad also had Fidel baptized in his Catholic church by the well-respected local Catholic priest of Tomegbe, Father Fidel Blewussi, after whom my brother was named. My dad was showing his devotion to his two religions by having the two ceremonies as well as by giving his baby boy the two names—the traditional Kable and the Christian Fidel.

Two, three, four months passed and nothing happened to Fidel; he remained very healthy. My parents eventually became convinced that this baby had come to stay. Maybe this baby had been "bought" from the hands of the family's enemies. Maybe the traditional ceremony was paying off, successfully protecting Fidel from the voodoo curses of the past. My father became happier with each passing day and was able for the first time to focus on how to provide for his wife and two children. Putting food on the family table became my dad's daily concern.

My father's relatives in Tomegbe gave him an efficiency room that he used as his first tailor shop. A certified tailor can start working on his own by buying a sewing machine or by renting one from a retired tailor or by working in partnership with friends or family.

Being a tailor in West Africa can be a profitable profession if one works hard and gives customers full satisfaction. Yes, anybody can be successful as long as he/she is loyal to his/her customers and sews well because African tailor-made clothes are affordable for the average person. While some luxurious fabrics are imported from European countries such as Holland, they cost twice or more as much as the locally manufactured fabrics.

There are local textile factories throughout West Africa. Fabrics from these factories made into African clothes by local tailors are cheaper and more popular in West Africa than factory-made clothes; the latter can only be found for sale in Western-style shops. Only a few Africans, mostly clerks living in big cities, wear or can afford expensive European-made clothes. The vast majority of Africans prefer to wear African-made clothes, cut and sewn by their favorite tailors. With the African-made clothes, the customer can choose the fabric as well as the style of the outfit. Yes, tailoring can be a profitable profession.

A couple of months after my dad opened his tailor shop, he became well known as one of the best tailors in Tomegbe. He was faithful and nice to his customers, always trying to give them 100 percent satisfaction. Not long after opening the shop, his business was booming at such a rate that the efficiency became too small for the shop, so my father rented a bigger room. With his good reputation spreading throughout the village, my dad was able to get more customers than he could handle; also, he was able to afford to take better care of his young family.

Like any tailor in Togo, my father's busiest and best season was the holiday season, known back home as Christmastime, which includes celebrating the New Year. These two holidays are by far the most joyful and most celebrated holidays in my country, and may I say that like many other people back home, Christmas has always been my favorite holiday.

In Togo, Christmastime is a family season. It is the only time of the year when everyone wants to be with their families; it is a big event for the Togolese. The season has always been celebrated with special fervor in the Western part of the country in the prefectures of Kloto, Amou (my own) Ogou, and by far the greatest celebration takes place in Wawa County where my parents were living at the time.

Christmas was celebrated more in these prefectures because, first of all, it is here that the highest percentage of Christians live. A second reason is that those four counties combined contain 90 percent of the most fertile farmland of Togo. They are the only part of Togo where cocoa and coffee are cultivated. After phosphate mining, which happens in the south of Togo, by the Atlantic Ocean. These crops provide the Togolese with their second largest source of revenue. Consequently, these are the richest prefectures or counties in Togo.

Since the harvest season for cocoa and coffee happens to be around Christmastime (October through February), people have more money to spend on the holiday.

Among the four counties, Wawa, where my parents were living, is the richest. In Wawa county (populated by my Akposso tribe), 99 percent of the people are Christians, and the county has the biggest number of cocoa plantation owners in Togo.

During the '50s and '60s, plantation owners were so wealthy they could afford to send their smartest sons to private schools in Togo, even to Europe. They were able to accomplish this while farmers in other parts of the country were struggling to send their children to local public schools.

The people of Wawa county, because of the money they make on their cocoa plantations, are still widely known in Togo for spending money like kings. They spend money on things for their families, such as big houses, fancy shoes, gold jewelry, and nice clothes. Above all, they spend money on the very colorful and expensive kente cloth made in Ghana.

Even today, the beautiful kente cloth is associated with the culture of Wawa and with the Akposso tribe in particular. During the '50s, when Ghana was considered one of the most advanced countries in West Africa because of its culture, values, and other attributes, it was understandable that such a great nation would have a huge impact on its neighbors and their people. Living on the border with Ghana, my Akposso tribe is in constant contact with life there.

Kente cloth is handwoven, made of heavy all-cotton or silk thread of different colors and printed with a wide variety of symbols, which represent the pride and happiness of the Ghanaian people and their respect for the environment and their traditional kings and chiefs. These symbols include a chair, representing the throne of the kings or of the village chiefs. A cane may also appear, as it was used by kings and chiefs. Shoes, hands, or footprints can be abstract symbols of domestic life, and wildlife may represent the rain, sun, vegetation etc.

A piece of a man's kente cloth is rectangular, about seven feet wide and ten feet and six inches long, and is made up of long strips of handwoven cloth. It's worn with the long edge behind the right shoulder; the right hand holds one corner while the left hand holds the other. The cloth is flipped up over the left shoulder, and then the cloth over the left arm is rolled loosely up to the upper arm, forming a loose sleeve. The left side is then tucked in close to the body, and the whole thing can be lifted and adjusted for the correct length. Worn correctly, the kente covers the entire body, except for the right arm and shoulder. Though simple, the kente is elegant and stately; it is the best dress for formal occasions.

Today, some men wear Western-style clothing under the kente, but traditionally nothing is worn underneath. A fancy, open-work eyelet shirt can be worn underneath, but other styles of clothing are not appropriate. In addition, Western-style dress shoes or sport shoes can't be worn with kente. An African sandal is required—the fancier, the better—preferably with snakeskin trim. The most popular and fanciest kente shoe is made only in Ghana and known in my Akposso tribe as *onipabua*, a fancy and flat leather sandals, beach sandals style.

Kente cloth, expensive because it is handwoven, lasts for years when well taken care of. Kente cloth is more expensive in Togo than in Ghana because it is imported from Ghana. It's by far one of the most luxurious traditional outfits in West Africa. While some wealthy farmers can afford several kente clothes, others are lucky to afford one or two in an entire lifetime.

Two or three weeks before Christmas, during the first or second week of *advanto* or advent, parents seriously start thinking about how to celebrate the most joyful season of the year. Parents' thoughts go first to their children because Christmas is considered a family holiday, and children receive special consideration. Maybe this is because of the religious nature of the holiday itself, focusing on the birth of a baby, our savior Jesus Christ. Thinking about the children, the first things that parents think about are clothes and shoes. Children love to dress up. They may have a roomful of toys, but every time they wear nice, new clothes, the expression on their young faces is one of great joy.

During the second week of advent, parents go to the village marketplace, if there is one, or to a neighboring village to shop for shoes and fabric to be sewn by the family's favorite tailor. Families who are better off financially make purchases for both Christmas and the New Year at the same time. Families with less money can afford to buy only one set of clothes for both holidays.

*****

Like other tailors, my father was always busy during this special time of the year; it was a holiday of frenzied activity. Obviously, my dad made good money sewing for entire families, although he only sewed for the males of a family.

Those few weeks before Christmas up to New Year's Day were his busiest time of the year. My father got up very early in the morning and spent day and night at his sewing machine. He only allowed himself a twenty-minute lunch break and a half-hour dinner break.

My father was always more concerned about getting his customers' orders ready on time and doing them well than on how much money he made from them. He always paid special attention to orders for children not only because the holidays were most special to them but because he felt that children were the most sensitive members of the family, and being a parent, my father was very sensitive to the feelings and the emotions of the little ones, especially during these holidays.

By giving 100 percent satisfaction to his customers, he was always reassured they would come back to him in the future.

Within a few months, because of his excellent work and positive work ethic, my dad's reputation had grown and spread fast, so fast that people in the village of Tomegbe with its population of nine hundred or so started calling my dad Tela for tailor instead of his real name and calling my mom Tela's wife. Both my dad and my mom were treated with respect and honor. My father's relatives in the village were very proud of my dad and mom for their accomplishments and for the positive impressions they have made on the people there.

Even today, whenever my parents visit Tomegbe, they always have a terrific time. People still greet them as "Tela and his wife." They left many positive impressions behind when they moved.

*****

In 1962, two years after Fidel was born, my mom had another baby boy. This baby was delivered on a Saturday evening in a small local clinic run by two European missionary nuns living in Tomegbe. That baby boy is the same person who thanks the Lord for His blessings and who is writing these lines today as his way of showing appreciation for what the good Lord, his parents, his family, his community, and his friends have given him.

Only five days after I was born, my parents received a letter from my dad's family in Agadji. The letter said that my father's uncle, head of the family in Agadji, was seriously ill and needed to be taken to the hospital. The family was convinced his illness was unusual because they had spent three months going from one voodoo priest to the next in search of a cure, but the sick man showed no sign of improvement. Clearly it was not a voodoo curse illness and couldn't be cured by a traditional medicine man. Their last hope was modern medicine, so they want to take him to the hospital in Kpalime (Palime), twenty-five miles from Agadji.

My father was called so he would come and be present before anything happened to his uncle. Back home, in such situations, people tend to put their animosities and differences behind them and try to express the true meaning of African community life by joining hands and efforts to face a tough situation. There's strength in unity, or as the French say, "L'union fait la force."

My father always cared a great deal about his family back home; he never lost sight of where he had come from no matter how comfortable he was becoming in Tomegbe. This letter that he received shortly before the start of the holiday season of the new year of 1963 presented my father with a great dilemma. Should he leave his wife and three children, especially his five-day-old baby, behind and go take care of his family's business? My dad's answer was a resounding, "No!" Since he had no idea how long he would have to stay in Agadji, as the letter only said the ill man needed to be taken to the hospital right away and not knowing how seriously ill his uncle was, my father couldn't tell whether his uncle was going to make it or not. Hopefully, he would survive, but my father realized that if his uncle died, he would have to stay even longer to arrange the burial ceremonies and funeral that, in my tribe, takes place several months to a year after the burial.

My father did not feel at ease with the idea of not going to the village. He simply could not live with himself if he stayed away, especially if his uncle died. If he moved himself and his family back to his native village, he would be ready for any eventuality without having to worry about having left his family behind in Tomegbe.

My poor dad had only twenty-four hours to make a decision, and there really was no choice. He spent day and night with my mom deciding on their best move.

My father would prefer not to leave Tomegbe so soon, where he was doing so well as a tailor after his long years of apprenticeship. His good reputation was spreading as fast as the wind in the Sahara desert. My father's young family's honor was growing as consistently as a baobab tree. He was enjoying serving people through his profession. He was finally enjoying his life among supportive relatives the way a person enjoys the first sunny day following a long, nasty winter.

My mother, like my father, was very skeptical about going back home. Here she was with three healthy children, including a newborn. Going back to Agadji, her husband's enemies might cause her to lose another child, especially her fragile newborn. My dear mother was scared to death of losing one of us; she was totally justified. It had happened twice before. Who in the world could reassure her that it would never happen again? Why move back, especially now that everything seemed to be going well for them in Tomegbe?

My father, driven by his deep affection for his uncle, knew he had to return to his native village, Agadji. As far as his family's security was concerned, he would put everything in God's hands. He managed to convince his wife that everything was going to be all right.

With a single mind, they decided to return to their native village, as if they all of sudden agreed with the French proverb "Le sejour d'un tronc d'arbre dans l'eau, ne le transformera pas en croquodile," meaning "No matter how long a piece of wood stays in the water or river, it will never become a crocodile." In other words, no matter how comfortable my parents were in Tomegbe, they still were originally from Agadji, and therefore, they would never become 100 percent people from Tomegbe; their home was in Agadji. The decision was made.

Uncomfortable and frightened of the unknown, my parents packed up their belongings, preparing to move the family back to their native village, Agadji.

While my dad knew this was the right thing to do, the decision to leave Tomegbe was a bitter pill for my dear parents to swallow. On top of it all, he now had the problem of convincing everyone else in Tomegbe of the rightness of the decision.

In the morning, my father went and told his Tomegbe relatives about the emergency and the uncertainties back home and that he and his wife had decided to move back to Agadji as soon as possible. Shocked by the sad news, my father's relatives couldn't believe their ears. They tried in vain to convince my dad that his wife and children's safety would be guaranteed if he left them behind. They also tried to convince my dad to leave his belongings behind and to come back to Tomegbe after he had taken care of the family business in Agadji. No matter what they tried, my father was ready to go. It was one of the saddest days for my dad, my mom, we three children, my father's relatives in Tomegbe, and my father's fast-growing group of customers. To some, my dad's departure was the loss of a relative; to others it was the loss of one of the best and most courteous tailors Tomegbe had ever known.

*****

My father, his wife, and their three children arrived in Agadji midafternoon on a quiet Sunday with all their belongings packed in a van. For my dad and my mom, the welcome they received was a mixture of sadness because of the illness in the family and joy at everyone seeing each other again.

My sister Pauline and my brother Fidel, respectively five and two, probably had the most painful change, having lost their playmates. As I was only a week or so old, the only important difference in my small world was a small one between my mom and my dad. To me, there was the familiar face of the person who breastfed me whenever I was hungry or crying and that of the other special person who played with me after I was full. Otherwise, I was unaffected by the move.

In Agadji, my dad didn't have a place of his own to stay because of the quick departure from Tomegbe, so his relatives in Agadji made room for his family in a one-bedroom apartment. This room was a little small for a family of five; unfortunately, it was the only space available.

Two days following our arrival in Agadji, my dad's uncle illness hadn't shown any sign of improvement. A family meeting was held. At that meeting, my father was selected to lead the delegation to take his uncle to a nearby hospital. The other members of my father's family stayed behind because his uncle was to be taken to the hospital in April the beginning of one of the busiest times for farmers in my region. It is the time to clean the farms up and to start planting new crops. Because my father had just arrived from Tomegbe, the family decided that he would be the least person to worry about any type of farming activity at that particular moment and, therefore, the best person to care for their ill relative in the hospital.

The morning after the meeting, my father took his uncle to Palime. Upon arrival at the hospital, tests were done immediately.

The illness was diagnosed. My grandfather, as I called him, was suffering from chronic testicular and prostate cancer.

My grandfather responded well to treatment in the beginning as if to prove our traditional African medicine wrong. Three weeks after entering the hospital, he showed significant signs of improvements. The doctor had warned my father that the treatments would probably take two to three months, so my father didn't get overly excited about his uncle's early signs of improvement. After two months, things were still going well, except that my grandfather still couldn't eat solid food; all he ate was soup every day.

My grandfather's attending physician felt sympathy for my father because he took on his shoulders the responsibility of caring for his uncle all by himself.

Truly this was an act of tremendous courage on my dad's part. Other family members would come to the hospital, and some would stay for a day or two, but my dad stayed with his uncle the entire time he was in the hospital.

During the third month in the hospital, my grandfather's health suddenly deteriorated. One day, before he entered a deep coma, never to regain consciousness, he called my dad to his bedside and thanked him for the good care he had given him. Then to my father's amazement, his uncle started confessing deep, dark secrets. He told my father that he was a wizard and that he had worked with others to kill my father's firstborn. "The decision to kill your baby," my grandfather continued, "was made by the family and intended to punish you for daring to argue with us over a piece of land." His uncle asked my father to forgive him.

He also told my dad that he felt so bad about his action that afterward he had decided to use his power to protect my dad's remaining children, especially me, the newborn baby.

My father, during his uncle's confession, asked him a very painful question, "How did you manage to kill my children from so far away?"

In answering this question, my grandfather revealed amazing secrets about witchcraft and how it works, secrets which are not known by the average person in my tribe. "A wizard or a witch," my grandfather said, "has the magical power that enables them to take different shapes at night. They can take the shape of snakes or dogs to bite their victims that live in the same village. However, most often, they take the shape of birds so that they can fly from one location to another. This is especially useful for faraway victims."

He told my father that the bird shape most commonly used by his fellow wizards and witches was that of an owl.

My grandfather also revealed that the favorite victims of wizards and witches are children between birth and age twenty because they are the most fragile ones, the most unprotected, and, therefore, the most vulnerable. "We," my grandfather continued, "usually operate in groups. As a bird or owl, we fly to the house of our victim at night when everyone, even the dogs, are sound asleep. At that time, we steal the soul of the victim. We usually land on the roof of the house and enter through the front door or by the window. Doors or windows don't have to be open. We go in and out whether they are open or closed. As soon as we are in possession of the soul of the victim, we fly back to our meeting place, where we usually decide when to kill the victim.

*****

That both wild bats and wild owls are hunted and eaten by my tribe might sound terrible to some Westerners, especially Americans, who would even be disgusted by the thought of them.

Cultural differences are interesting to me, especially to look at how something becomes defined as good or bad.

When it comes to food, the notion of good and bad varies greatly from one culture to another. While in India, for religious reasons, cows are revered, Westerners, especially Americans, can hardly live without their fast food hamburgers at places like McDonald's and Burger King. While Muslims, again for religious reasons, stay away from pork, most Americans eat sausages without thinking twice. While Japanese love their sushi, others prefer their fish cooked, even if they may like their beef raw. Some people eat cat meat, dog meat, horse meat, snake meat, and even frog legs—the variations seem endless. What makes it okay for some to eat frog legs, which are taboo in Africa?

Our reactions to others' eating habits is really nothing but a state of mind, influences from our environment and our society, period. Life might be easier for all of us if we realized these influences; sadly, we have the tendency of telling ourselves that life is only "okay" when others do it "our way."

"We transform our victims into an animal that people normally eat, such as goats, chicken, or sheep. We hide our victims in our secret dark room known only to group members or to other wizards and witches with whom we do business. As soon as we capture our victim," my dad's uncle declared, "and transform him/her into an animal, the real person starts getting sick, and if his/her family fails to get him/her away from us, the victim will certainly die the same day we kill the animal that represents him/her. Only members of the group," my grandfather added, "are allowed to eat meat from the animal."

Upon hearing this confession from the person whom for three months my dad had been caring for constantly, my father was very depressed. He kept thinking about the two children who had been taken away by his enemies with this uncle's help. Even though my father was still not sure about his second child's death, he had been convinced the first had been killed by my dad's family, a fact now verified by my father's uncle.

My grandfather's confession vividly reminded my dad of the night before the death of his first son.

Reliving the painful memories of the death of his child, several hours passed before my father regained his strength and could go on caring for his uncle.

My father was unable to show his uncle his anger. First of all, his uncle was dying. Second, my dad had already put the death of his two children behind him. Third, he didn't want to make any foolish move, such as getting upset and leaving the sick man by himself in a hospital bed. If he left his sick uncle there, my father would be throwing away any good will he would otherwise receive from his relatives for having stayed by his uncle all these months. My dad thought twice before acting foolishly. Somehow, he found the moral strength to finish the job he had begun, to stay till the end.

My father was indeed saddened, listening as his uncle confessed his sins. My dad was depressed; he was deeply drawn into the sad memories of that day in Tomegbe. However, my father built a wall between the past and the present, an attitude that prevented him from seeking revenge on his ill, vulnerable, and maybe dying uncle.

*****

My grandfather apologized to my father for having sent the owl to capture his baby's soul. Then, like many feeling the final hour drawing near, he wanted to put everything in order to prepare for the next long journey, so my grandfather gave my dad directions about the family's affairs. My grandfather made my father heir to any of his farms that my father wanted; he did this in appreciation for the care, love, and compassion my father had shown him during his final days, and especially for the forgiveness my father gave him.

Because his speech was slowed by his weakness, my grandfather's final speech took a long time. As soon as he finished, he slipped into a coma from which he never regained consciousness; he passed away at six thirty that evening in September 1963. With his uncle's death, my father laid aside the bitterness from the bad memories. For someone like my father, who had missed the privilege of growing up with his real father, his uncle was very important to him. No matter what he had done, he was still the only strong male figure that my father had known as a child. It was unfortunate that this same uncle had hurt him by taking part in the killing of my father's son, his own grandson.

Without wasting any time, my dad arranged for an ambulance to take the body of his beloved uncle home to Agadji the following day. Then he left for Agadji himself to tell the family, the village, and the surrounding villages the sad news—that the head of the family, Mr. Edoh Kpalaka, had died.

All his life, my father had based his behavior on a very simple philosophy, namely, "If you do something, make sure you do it right." My father, so far, had been doing everything right. He had spent three months in the hospital taking care of his uncle. He had forgiven this uncle for what he had done to his family, and he had arranged for his uncle's body to be transported safely back to the village.

Out of respect for his community, my father arrived prior to his uncle's body to alert everyone and to make final arrangements so that the burial ceremonies and other traditional ceremonies in honor of the deceased would go well. Having done all that was required by tradition, my dad was at peace with himself and was convinced that he would receive the much-needed help to complete the tasks of digging the grave at the cemetery, building temporary shelters to house visitors and other relatives, and cooking food.

It's widely said that Africans live a communal life, and sharing and helping seem to be a natural part of life. Helping each other is just what is done. Some critics in the world outside of Africa suggest that this is not true and that instead, Africans are more likely than anyone else to spend our time killing, starving, and performing atrocities on one another. True, there are problems. Let's look at a few reasons for this.

One fundamental reason for political problems in Africa is that when the European colonizers landed in Africa, they didn't care or pay attention to who was living where or to whom got along with whom. As a result, they often created nations where groups of peoples who were long-standing enemies were forced to become "countrymen."

A power struggle in Africa means a struggle for survival because in African countries, the group in power most often oppresses and abuses "outsiders." Such behavior has resulted in horrors described in the news. In Eastern Africa in the 1980s, the civil war in Ethiopia led to the mass starvation of Ethiopians. Ethiopia had once been supported and exploited by Italy and at another time by the former USSR. Eritrea, colonized by Italy, had been forced into a union with Ethiopia. This "civil war," which cost so many lives, were about Eritrea and Ethiopia trying to separate back into independent groups.

Further south, in Mozambique and Angola, civil wars were organized and fueled behind the scene both by the United States government fighting a "communist" regime and by European countries trying to maintain their own interests in the region. The starvation of children and adults in Somalia and their slaughter in the wars in Liberia and in Ruwanda between the Hutus and Tutchis, to name only a few, further illustrate the disastrous results of the struggles for power among tribes.

The negative images of these conflicts on Western television have led some to conclude that these terrible events only occur in Africa. Nothing could be further from the truth. There are many stories throughout the history of Europe, especially about the World Wars I and II; can anything equal the Holocaust visited upon the Jewish people under Hitler? Even today, wars continue in the former Yugoslavia between the Serbs, the Croats and the Muslims. Outrages being perpetuated there are no less ferocious than in Africa.

Perhaps what we see in all these areas of the world is actually a human problem. Sadly, we human beings, whether white, yellow, black, or Red, though supposedly blessed with better brain cells than animals, seem to like to fight, hurt, and kill each other. The stronger misuses his/her power to take advantage of the weak and poor, as wild animals do in the jungle. The main difference between ourselves and the animals is that they fight and kill out of necessity; we seem to enjoy the violence. Sometimes, animals get along better than we human beings.

When it comes to using our intellect to live in peace with one another regardless of race and skin colors, we humans don't do well at all.

Regardless of how much or how often we Africans fight among ourselves, we highly value community life and living communally. Events, such as marriages and funerals, are occasions when Africans show this spirit. When someone is getting married, it's more than one person or one family's celebration; by the same token, when a person dies, it's more than one family's burden. The whole village comes together as one to face the situation, to share the pain or the joy.

*****

Knowing and respecting this general African way of life that my tribe especially followed, my father did everything expected of him, and it paid off.

On Saturday morning, following the announcement by my dad of his uncle's death, the entire village started preparations for the burial ceremonies. First thing in the morning, close friends and relatives came to present their deepest sympathy and to weep with the deceased's family.

During a funeral, it becomes clear how daily life is organized and segregated based on age and sex among my people.

As is the custom in all deaths of our villagers, the older men and husbands took up hoes, axes, pickaxes, shovels, and machetes and headed to the cemetery to dig the grave while the younger men grabbed their machetes and headed to the forest to bring back large quantities of palm branches and wood from special trees to make a shelter for the visitors. The shelter was built near the compound of the deceased's family by young adults under the supervision of the elderly men. It is amazing how fast these shelters can be built. These young men grow up to be truly expert builders, thanks to their involvement in the routine.

While today, thanks to the charity of the French Catholic priests, Fathers Jean Paul Felder and Cochere, my village has public running water. At the time of my father's uncle's death, the river was the only source. Therefore, girls and young women walked the mile to supply water to the deceased's family to be used in cooking. Watching these women carrying buckets and huge pans full of water back to the village on their head is always an amazingly beautiful sight. Upon watching them, the first question from a Westerner is often, "How the hell do they do that?" Well, Mother Africa is truly a mother of necessity; we do what we have to do, and the result is often beautiful.

Meanwhile, the elderly women headed to the deceased's family's compound and began building the mud stoves that they would use to cook meals for all attending the burial ceremonies. There would be people coming from the surrounding villages and from far away.

In a developing country, like Togo, where telephones still have not reached the average person, information somehow manages to circulate rapidly both within a village and between villages, especially when the person involved is famous or popular.

The digging of the grave and the building of stoves and shelters required several long hours. Supplying the water, the women made several trips to the river. All these activities—digging the grave, building shelters and stoves, and getting in supplies of firewood and water—were completed early in the morning.

Usually almost all in the village participate in these "self-help" activities. I call them self-help because in Africa, we also say "what goes around comes around." The more often an individual helps fellow villagers, the more help that individual receives in turn. Those who do not participate have good reasons. They might be sick or have a sick person in their home. They might have a newborn. Any good reason is understood and accepted. In tiny villages like mine, where everybody knows everybody's business, there is little room for faked excuses.

As soon as the firewood and water were collected, women started collecting and preparing the grains for cooking. The grains are corn, rice, beans (red, black, and white), and fonio (a typical Akposso traditional grain similar in size and shape to couscous).

Because of their experience, the elderly women supervise the entire operation. Some "helpers" were directed to take corn to the local mill to be made into flour; others went to work to prepare the rice and fonio.

In my village, there are only two kinds of mills—one for coffee and one for corn. All other foods that require processing prior to cooking are processed by hand.

Rice and beans, which have been stored in mud silos near the living quarters, are taken out and spread in thin layers on zinc roofing sheet to help dry it a little. The fonio is fried in special large pans and cooled.

When the grains are ready to be pounded, they are taken either to the deceased's family's compound or to a place called in Akposso *Odjani*, a word I find difficult to translate into English. Odjani contains the village's sacred trees; these trees are either in the center of the village or in the original center of the village. This place is filled with traditional power; this meeting place was chosen by the founding fathers of the village as a place where traditional ceremonies would occur and decision important to the village would be made.

The pounding of grains, such as rice, beans, and fonio, into meal is done with two tools: a mortar and a pestle. Both pestle and mortar are handmade from a special wood. The mortar, being more difficult to make, takes longer to carve than the pestle. The mortar is two to three feet high and between twenty to twenty-five inches wide. The pestle, often as long as five feet, is wider (about six or seven inches round) at each end than the in-between section (about three or four inches round). The pestle, to some extent, is shaped like a baseball bat but is longer. The pestle is reversible, with one end the right thickness for pounding yams for "foo foo" and the other the right size for husking rice. The middle of the pestle is thinner, making it easier to grasp. While the pounding process requires only one or two people, up to four can be involved at once.

During occasions like funerals, when huge amounts of grains are waiting to be husked, there is no time to waste, and the same mortar is shared by three or four people. To do that, a very strict rhythm is followed by the pounders; each person is assigned a number (#1, #2, #3, or #4) to follow, like the rhythm a conductor sets up for an orchestra. When two people share a mortar, the rhythm is "one-two, one-two" back and forth. Three people form a triangle and use a one-two-three rhythm, and four people form a square and use a one-two-three-four rhythm. While the sight of these activities is beautiful, the rhythm of the pestles combined with the women's sensuous voices singing songs, which vary with the occasion, is incredible.

The pounding requires lifting the pestle with both hands as high as possible and bringing it down as hard as possible on the grain to be pounded. Sometimes women can be seen switching the pestle from one hand to the other. This movement is repeatedly done until the work is finished. The pounding is very tiring but at the same time is good for building the body's strength.

Another labor the women do is separating the good grain from the bad as well as separating the seed from the peel or husk. This task is usually done by the elderly who are too tired or weak to pound the grains. As in the construction of stoves and shelters, the separating of good and bad grains requires talent and experience.

Separating the meal from the husk is a very slow, complex process. A small amount of pounded grain is put on a flat and round wood plate that is about an arm's length in size. Once the grain has been pounded, the husk is loosened from the grain. To separate the two, the women repeatedly throw the mixture into the air. If there is a light breeze, the husk is easily blown away while the heavier grain falls back onto the basket. Finally, the good grain is ready to be cooked.

*****

When the food preparation was completed, the Odjani was swept clean; in fact, in preparation for the funeral ceremonies, it was left in better condition after the cleanup than it was before the pounding activities had taken place. The Odjani must be kept clean at all times because it is a sacred place where the most important traditional ceremonies are held.

By the time the women were done pounding the grains, the men had finished digging the grave and were returning home from the cemetery, which was about a mile or two from the village. For a few hours, the entire village returned to its calm life, during which time people cleaned their own homes to house the guests who would start arriving in the evening. This cleaning, too, is important because, in addition to staying with the deceased's family, guests stayed with whomever they knew or wherever there was room in the village. It's important that people's homes be prepared for the possibility of guests and strangers.

*****

When my grandfather died, the number of villagers who participated in the ceremonies was very large. Everybody seemed to give my father good marks for the way he had handled the situation so far, and they responded to his calls for help with enthusiasm. My dad supervised the entire operation. He oversaw every activity. He spent time with everybody—the women at their stove building and food preparation and the men at the cemetery digging the grave. When we were all ready and the villages had gone to prepare their own homes, my dad left my mother in charge and returned to the hospital accompanied by a few members of the family to bring his uncle's body home.

The village was peaceful, grieving for my father's uncle. The only sounds were the songs, cries, and laughter of children too young to understand the mood of the villagers. Once in a while, parents tried to silence their little ones, but they didn't understand why everybody else was so quiet. To them, their parents' sudden harsh behavior toward them was hard to comprehend. Unfortunately, in Africa, lessons are most often learned by observation, so few adults took the time to explain what was happening. Then children could only guess that maybe everyone was having a bad day.

At 5:15 p.m., the small village of Agadji was shaken awake by the earsplitting sounds of an ambulance's siren. Every curious eye popped out to see what was going on. The multicolored headlights were flashing with such a brightness that some villagers were unable to look at them. The rare sight of an ambulance stopping in the village brought a mixture of emotions: sadness and fear.

Because Agadji is located on International Route #2 between the two cities, Atakpame and Kpalime, and the capital city of Lome, the villagers see a lot of traffic every day, both the regular traffic such as trucks, buses, and taxis and irregular traffic such as ambulances, so some people hardly give the traffic a second look. However, ambulances in the past with their flashing lights were making their way to the hospitals of Atakpame and Kpalime. The villagers had never seen an ambulance come to and stop in Agadji itself.

*****

In my village, people have never really gotten used to the sight or sounds of ambulances. Ambulances are seen as the carriers of bad news, as evil as witches, wizards, or owls. Ambulances symbolize illness and death—the two worst enemies of human beings. I find it ironic that my Akposso tribe worships their dead through animism or voodoo and at the same time fear ambulances because they transport the dead.

These fears extend to the ambulance drivers. The villagers of my tribe avoid and fear the drivers, even if these men are their friends. Furthermore, the ambulance drivers fear the dead so much that they perform rituals for protection before transporting the dead. During a traditional ceremony, two fresh eggs are placed in front of the front tires of the ambulance (one in front of each front tire). When the ambulance moves forward, the eggs are crushed. The ceremony is performed both when the ambulance leaves with a body and after the body has been dropped off. This ceremony is supposed to give protection to the driver and clear his way to his final destination and back to the hospital.

*****

In addition, the ambulance stopping in the village was a sight to remember because in my father's time, few villagers could afford to send their sick relatives to hospitals. Sick people were usually treated at home.

If a relative was sent to a hospital, the ambulance, which had only recently been introduced into the rural areas. had to be rented, and few people could afford the cost.

If people thought they could make it to the hospital before death struck, they would rent a cab, a much cheaper way of transporting bodies, dead or alive, than in ambulances. Exactly why my dad rented an ambulance, which was most expensive and which scared the whole village, is unclear. Perhaps he did it to show how capable he was or because of his concern about doing the right thing.

The truth in my tribe is that, even though a funeral is a sad event, it is also an opportunity to be fashionable and spend a lot of money. The idea behind the extravagant spending is to show the whole community how much the dead person was loved. Even if loans or the sale of land is necessary, an attempt is made to create an event that will become the most memorable of times. Yes, too much money is spent by my people on funerals, money that villagers just don't have. Too often, a family becomes broke putting on a funeral. The younger generation honestly thinks that it's nonsense to spend money we don't have on dead people while the living people have too many financial problems.

Another sad reality is that people often spend more money on a person's funeral than they did to keep the person alive.

As if to remind us of this nonsense, one of the most popular songs in the southern part of Togo says, "We, human beings have the tendency of loving the dead more than those who are still alive." My dad's family was no exception to this rule. True, the family had gotten together to raise the funds to send my father's uncle to the hospital, but my father was the only family member to care for his uncle at the hospital for those three long months. While the family followed the rule, if it's true that there is no rule without an exception, then maybe here my father was the exception. Like the other family members, he was spending a lot of money on his dead uncle's funeral, but my father had also given much of himself during his uncle's long illness, and everybody in the village, including his now dead uncle, knew it. My father had loved his uncle when he was healthy, and he had loved him when he was ill, so much so that my father had given up everything in Tomegbe and moved to Agadji to spend those last three months with his uncle in the hospital. My dad also loved his uncle after death, which is why he wanted to show him all the honor and respect he deserved by making his burial ceremonies and funeral successful and, more importantly, memorable.

In renting the expensive ambulance, my father was just trying to do the right thing.

As soon as the ambulance pulled over, my father got out. Seeing tears rolling down her husband's face, my mother couldn't hold back her own. She started crying, setting the tone for an open expression of sympathy for my dad, his uncle, and the deceased's family by villagers and guests.

The villagers who had settled into a quiet mood after completing the preceremony preparations were about to be transformed.

Suddenly, the atmosphere became tense, the air full of sadness and cries. The children who earlier were happy and seemed not to care about much couldn't understand why everybody, including their own parents, was suddenly crying their eyes out. Those children who were sensitive or very attached to their parents started crying, too, without knowing the reason.

When a person dies in my tribe, it's very important that you cry sincerely to show how much love and respect you have for the dead and the deceased's family. Villagers watch one another very closely when it comes to showing sympathy. No cries should be faked. People in my tribe say, "Do not cry the way Westerners do with handkerchiefs in their hands to make it look like they are really crying." No. Faked cries are not allowed in my tribe. When a person cries during a death, wake, or funeral, everybody wants to see real tears cascading down their cheeks, the way water flows over Niagara Falls in the United States and Canada (only that is considered a real cry in my tribe).

As I said, everybody was crying, except for some teenagers who had not yet learned to cry sincerely or who wanted to remain "cool" by not crying. Because of their age, adolescents can escape the social pressure to cry for a while. However, the older they become, the closer they are watched, so older teens have no choice but to do the right thing and cry well, whether they like it or not. They must show respect for their friends and their friends' families.

In my tribe, it's commonly acceptable for women to cry. Men usually don't cry, or rather, don't cry easily. Men are supposed to be the role models of the family, the ones with broader shoulders and iron hearts, the ones that are supposed to take any heat without crying for help. A man must be morally, physically, psychologically, and emotionally strong. When a man cries, something serious must have happened to him. On very rare occasions like funerals, men do cry; it is a time that men can show that they, too, have hearts and feelings. I've seen strong men in my village cry their eyes out like whipped babies.

On that sad day, the loss of his dear uncle affected my father greatly, so much that he cried like a baby. As the crying was still going on, about six previously selected strong adult males entered the ambulance to remove the body. A few minutes after the body was taken out, the ambulance returned to the hospital in Kpalime from where the little devil had come. The expression on everybody's face was of deep relief—relief that said, "Oof! Thank you for going back to the hell you came from!"

Before my father arrived with his uncle's body in the ambulance, my mother had arranged with her in-laws for a place to take the deceased's body, so the body was taken to that location where the temperature was cooler near the deceased's family compound. In Togo, and certainly in my village, Agadji, there is no such business as a funeral home. Each family is intimately responsible for their dead. Everything including the coffin, the outfit to be worn by the dead, even the last bath given to the dead, has to be taken care of or done by the deceased's family.

In my Akposso tribe, the last bath is usually given by elderly women chosen by the deceased's family based on their close relationship with the family and experience in such matters. Regardless of the age or sex of the dead, the last bath and dressing are done only by these elderly women. Why do women usually have to do the most complex and dirty jobs, one might ask. In this case, women are given the responsibility in order to show respect to our mothers, to all women. Yes, no matter how tough or famous an individual is when alive, whether the person was once rich and powerful or very poor, when the person dies, in my tribe, they return to the care of women. After all, the unshakable truth is, we are all born by women, come into the world through women, and therefore, we return to the other world with the help of women. Yes, those humble creatures too often don't get the credit they truly deserve, or they are simply taken for granted by their macho male counterparts.

Guests started pouring into Agadji shortly after the body arrived, as if they had purposely waited for the departure of the ambulance, most of them coming on foot from the surrounding villages; they came bearing gifts. The women carried on their head firewood, which they gave to the deceased's family as a gesture of sympathy and burden sharing. Male guests made financial contributions.

Because the community wanted to be certain that all guests arrived in the village, they stopped at the deceased's family's home with their contributions. Contributions might also be sent to the deceased's family through friends or relatives if a person could not make it to the funeral. The gifts range from a few cents to a quarter, depending on each person's capacity to contribute. In a society like ours, where community life is the soul of the people, it's very important that everybody participates, regardless of the quantity or the quality of the contribution; what really matters is participating, as it shows that a person cares and is part of the community.

Contributions are conscientiously recorded in a special notebook that the head of the deceased's family opened prior to the arrival of the guests. The person who registers the names of the donors, their village or origin, and the place they were staying in the village is called the secretary.

This secretary is a trusted member of the family and might be the most educated person in the family or the village or a trusted relative from another village.

*****

My grandfather was over eighty when he passed away. Anytime a man of that age or older dies, the ceremonies are always extraordinary, and so it was with my grandfather's.

Though the villagers had already learned of Mr. Edoh Kpalaka's death, they were waiting for the official traditional announcement. It came at 6:00 p.m. A powerful, seven-gun salute was fired by selected dignitaries of the village from the Odjani. The gun salute was followed by the always beautiful sound of the traditional drum called Atupani.

Atupani is a gigantic wooden drum (about two and half meters long and fifteen inches wide) with a unique importance to my tribe. Atupani plays the role of the modern telephone and is only played on special occasions, such as at the death of an elderly man like my grandfather, Edoh K., or during war. The Atupani is used to spread news, usually bad; in a sense, it is used like a modern warning siren.

Atupani, also called the talking drum, can only be played by chosen elderly people. It cannot be played with like an ordinary drum. The person who beats the Atupani uses specifically coded sounds to announce what was going on. These sounds mimic the tones of our language. Only elderly people understand and can translate these coded sounds into the language spoken by the average person.

Atupani is very powerful and it attracts the souls of the dead. Whenever the Atupani is being played, the dead can come back through their relatives who go into trance.

Witnessing the transformation of fellow villagers in trance can cause one to question, if not lose for good, their Christian beliefs. It is impossible to deny this African reality happening right before one's eyes. That reality is very strong and can shake one's hold or sense of the world so hard that an individual may wonder if they are daydreaming or perhaps have been transported to another planet.

As the soul of the dead enters its relative, it makes the person lose total control of his or her senses, and the person starts acting exactly like the dead relative who is coming back for a visit. Persons in trance are closely watched by other relatives, for they can act totally crazy and weird. For instance, people in trance might take off their clothes and run around totally naked without concern.

The dead enter their relatives without warning, so the person chosen to be possessed is caught by surprise. The dead may enter a person at any time—when they are eating, cooking, taking a shower, or sleeping. The persons chosen by the dead are usually the best behaved individuals in the village, and most of the time they are women.

While those in trance start by acting weird, as if to attract the audience's attention, the dead do not come back only to act crazy; they also return to help solve the family's problems. It isn't until the villagers start paying close attention to those in trance that they start talking, delivering the messages from the dead and telling the living the reason for their visit.

What the persons in trance talk about is so accurate that it is impossible to remain skeptical or be suspicious that the messengers are making their demands up. For instance, a person in trance might tell family member A to stop being rude to a particular family member, family member B to go ahead and adopt a particular cousin in a particular village, family member C to let go of a particular piece of land, family member D to stop causing trouble in the family, or else. In fact, the dead have even been known to threaten to kill major troublemakers in a family.

I myself have experienced this African reality. Many times I remember seeing my own mother acting exactly like those tranced messengers I have described. I have seen my own mother acting weird and crazy, very close to taking her clothes off. How embarrassing that would had been for me to see my mother naked in public!

Once in 1974, during the funeral of my mother's favorite uncle, Mr. Melesusu Essousso, I saw my mother go into trance. How often this has happened to my mom, I don't know. My father, however, has never been affected by the drum in this way.

*****

The Atupani drum was removed from the Odjani and taken to its secret hiding place as soon as it had officially announced my grandfather's death. Room was made in the Odjani for the meeting that would be held by all the elderly people present in the village.

Several hours passed before the most conservative guests of all started arriving. These were the keepers of our Akposso traditions, the elderly people, "the wise ones." Their coming together began with a traditional prayer and libation in honor of all the village's dead and for the well-being of the village itself.

While this ceremony was being performed at the Odjani, women were cooking dinner for the guests. Following dinner, people prepared to sit up all night. Tea, coffee, and hot chocolate would be served. Small traditional singing and dancing groups were organized for the evening. One group was the village chorus of the St. Augustine Church. This group, of which my mother is still a member, sang beautiful religious songs and read beautiful Bible verses to attract nonbelievers.

The wake started around 8:00 p.m. and continued until dawn. During the night, while everybody was being entertained and kept awake by entertainers, a group of four elderly women took my grandfather away for his last bath. Before those waiting knew it, my grandfather had been cleaned and laid out for display in a white long gown, looking like an angel or like the altar boys who help the priests during the mass. My grandfather had such a relaxed expression on his face. Maybe he was happy to see his relatives, including his parents in the "other" world. Maybe he was relieved to have apologized to my father for his part in killing his baby. Or maybe he was simply satisfied that his death had finally and peacefully taken away his sufferings and removed the heavy burden that his long illness had imposed on his family, and especially my father. Only Mr. Edoh could have explained the real reason for the expression on his face. In any case, no one could tell he had been ill for a long time prior to his death.

Before the sun rose, around five thirty, the deceased's family's compound was empty. Everybody had returned home with their heads and eyes filled with thoughts of sleep. Everyone who had been working nonstop since the day before looked very tired. The wake had taken their last energy, but they all kept on going because some guests who hadn't made it to the village the day before were just arriving.

The next day was Sunday, and those who didn't have specific tasks took time off and went to church. Around nine that morning, the females resumed their cooking, this time for lunch. Females are always in charge of cooking. The whole village smelled good because of the cooking being done in all the households. At eleven, lunch was ready to be served.

Because the guests were spread throughout the village, females transported the meal, moving about quickly, displaying their endurance and art of moving. The food was served in flat, round pans that the females balanced on their heads. They walked from one place to another, from one family to another, any place a guest might be staying.

As is the custom, following lunch, the whole village returned to the deceased's family compound for a final viewing of my grandfather's body and to pay tribute to him before he was put in his coffin and taken away to be buried. Only adults and mature teenagers were allowed to view the dead with children kept away to prevent them from having nightmares.

While the viewing of the body was going on, small groups formed again to entertain the crowd one last time before the burial ceremonies. The burial time varies. Because bodies are not embalmed, they can deteriorate quickly in hot environment. During the dry season, when the temperature goes up to 80 degrees and beyond, burials usually happen in the morning or early afternoon.

As my grandfather died in mid-June, the beginning of the rainy season, the temperature was cooler; in addition, his body had been kept in a morgue for twenty-four hours, so the viewing could last longer.

Even though my dad's dead uncle had lived a double religious life, being Catholic and animist, he managed to keep his records clean and straight as far as the Catholic Church was concerned. He followed most of the Catholic teachings, such as paying the annual tithe to the church, being baptized, and having his first communion. As a result, he was allowed to be buried in the Catholic cemetery by a Catholic priest. Had he not kept his religious records straight, he would have been buried with the "nonbelievers."

At three in the afternoon, the church bells at St. Augustine Church started ringing, signaling that it was time to take the body there. My grandfather was put in the nice coffin that my father and his family had ordered from Atakpame. In the coffin, relatives put extra shoes and clothes to supply the dead on his journey to his final home. In my tribe, it's very important to include these items because we believe in life after death and reincarnation. We believe the dead are not really dead; only their bodies leave while the soul is still alive.

As soon as the coffin was closed, six strong adult men, three for each side, were chosen to carry it to the church. Because the deceased's compound was only a mile from the church, the walk to the church took only twenty minutes. Behind the coffin walked the immediate family members of the deceased, and they were followed by the chorus and then by the villagers and guests; everyone was wearing white shirts.

Normally in my tribe, black symbolizes sorrow, fear, or darkness, while white symbolizes joy, happiness, and peace. Under normal circumstances, when a person dies, everybody attending the funeral or burial ceremonies is required to wear black or something dark, close to black. However, on rare occasions, when a person of my grandfather's age passes away, people are asked to wear white. The reason is very simple: the elderly person is thought to be returning to his or her original home. He or she had lived long enough to be tired of life and is returning to the Creator. Hence, we the living should not feel sorry for or mourn them. Maybe that was one reason why my grandfather looked so relieved and had that peaceful, relaxed expression on his face.

The final prayer at the church was short, and then the procession moved to the cemetery with the coffin. As soon as the burial ceremonies there ended, everybody went back to the village except for a dozen men chosen to remain behind to fill in the grave. Upon returning to the village, some began their trip home, while others helped clean up and organize things at the deceased's home.

At six o'clock, one of my dad's nephews was given a gong by the head of the family. He sounded the gong to invite mostly the adult males, villagers and guests, to a drinking session at the Odjani. Among the Akposso, it's socially acceptable for a man to drink in public, but not women. Hence, 99.9 percent of the people going to the party were men. The very few women who went were sixty years old or older. The drink most often served is local palm wine.

Palm trees are of special importance and are widely grown in Togo and particularly in the Southwestern region.

Planting palm trees is like planting apple, mango, or orange trees; they don't grow overnight. It takes five years or more for a palm tree to be really productive. When the tree matures, its leaves are used to make brooms and woven mats; its branches and leaves are used to make shelters, such as those built during funerals; and its branches are used to make all sizes of baskets and to build grain silos.

Mature palm trees also produce palm nuts. When the palm nut is ripe, its fire red skin is used to cook palm sauce, which is one of my favorite meals and is truly delicious. Red palm oil is also made from the nut. In the nut is a core that is used to make another cooking oil, which is black.

Both the red and black cooking oils are used to make a popular traditional soap.

In its seventh year, the palm tree can be used to make palm wine. During the dry season, the palm tree is cut down or hollowed out. Four to five days later, the tree is cleared of branches, and a five- or ten-inch wide square hole about six inches deep is cut at the base of the branches where palm nuts form. The hole is covered with bark to keep the inside of the tree warm; the warmer it is inside the tree, the more wine is produced, just as when we wear warm clothes we sweat. Palm wine is nothing more than the sweet sweat from the heart of the palm tree.

In the middle of this hole, at the bottom, a round, finger-sized hole is opened and connected with a bamboo spout to a small container placed under the tree.

Every evening, the sheets of bark are removed and the hole is steamed with dry, clean branches to increase the temperature inside the tree. The area is then cleaned and recovered with the bark. This is done regularly until the tree stops producing.

Once or twice a day, depending on the productivity of the tree, containers are emptied of their wine, which is transported to local markets for sale and consumption. The wine produced during the first four or five days, which is called Tukumu in Akposso, is sugar sweet and contains a relatively low concentration of alcohol. The longer the tree produces, the older the wine and the higher the concentration of alcohol.

From palm wine, a strong brandy-like liquor can be made. The process is as follows: the day's wine is collected from the trees and poured into a big tank and left to ferment until the tree is out of wine (usually three to four weeks). When the fermentation is complete, the tank full of wine is carefully placed on a stove and boiled. Next to the fermented wine tank are others filled with constantly cold water. Next to the tanks of cold water is a jar into which runs a funnel that has a cotton filter.

The tank containing the boiling, fermented wine is sealed while those containing the cold water are open to the air. A metal pipe that connects the boiling tank to the jar runs through the cold water. The cold water plays the most important role of cooling the alcohol, which comes out of the boiling tank in the form of steam by condensing it back into liquid—in this case, a liquor. Slowly, the liquid drips into the jar, filtering through the cotton. The process is time-consuming; the dripping continues twelve hours every day.

The final product is a liquor, much stronger than whisky and vodka, called Sodabi. Sodabi can also be repossessed to obtain an even stronger liquor called Zota. Regular palm wine is relatively slow to turn a drinker's head or brain upside down; however, Sodabi does not play around, and Zota can be dangerous if abused.

*****

During the drinking at the Odjani, where the younger men wait on the elderly men, only the regular palm wine and Sodabi were served—for financial reasons, I'm sure. Palm wine is quite inexpensive, and while Sodabi is quite expensive, reflecting the difference in price, regular palm wine is served in a twenty-ounce calabash and Sodabi in a much smaller glass. Zota is simply too expensive for most occasions.

The drinking is not to celebrate the death; instead, it fulfills the role of a male social gathering at the closing of the burial ceremonies. During this drinking session, the elderly men set a date for the actual funeral designed as a time to remember the dead. The funeral usually takes place within two to six months, though it may be put off for up to a year, depending on the deceased's family's agenda. Sometimes families combine the funerals of two or three dead relatives to save money and time.

Nobody goes to the closing ceremonies with the intention of getting drunk; even villagers like my father who don't drink alcohol attend these ceremonies.

While men were busy drinking their last drop, women were busy gossiping and getting ready to head back to their villages. One thing women never forget to take home with them is leftovers from a funeral for any children who had to stay back home, and there is always plenty of food left over no matter how poor the deceased's family is.

This, once more, shows how much money is spent on burial ceremonies. Perhaps, my people ought to cut back some on the money they spend at these events, but spending money is a way of showing their love for their beloved deceased.

Before darkness had covered Agadji with its scary, thick, sad, black sheet, all guests had returned to their own villages. Agadji was once again shrunk to its normal population of about one thousand inhabitants. While my mother was still finishing chores in the household, my father was exhausted. He took a hot shower, sat down in the living room, and, a few minutes later, fell asleep.

Monday, the next morning, before sunrise, a meeting was held at the head of our family's house. Following the meeting, even before the villagers had a chance to return to their daily activities, my dad and his family, including my mom, were going from house to house, door to door, as is the custom, to thank the villagers for their help, support, and contributions to the deceased's families. Then later that day, letters were written and sent to the village leaders and priests in the surrounding villages to thank all for their help and participation.

It wasn't until a week later that my father started recovering from the sadness and fatigue that had accumulated during the tense days of the burial ceremonies. For the first time since he had moved his three children and wife back from Tomegbe, he started readjusting to day-to-day life in Agadji.

Although before long we all had adjusted to our new home, environment, and friends, Pauline and Fidel, like many kids, adjusted to our new life and new friends faster than our parents did. Our immediate cousins became their fast friends, and life in Agadji was soon not very different for them from their old life in Tomegbe. What a betrayal of their old friends in Tomegbe! Not really! Pauline and Fidel were too busy making new friends and too young to really think about betraying anyone. As for me, life didn't change. Being a baby, it really didn't matter where I was, whether in Agadji, Tomegbe, or Paris, as long as I had my parents, who were my whole world.

My father, his wife, and three children were still in that one-bedroom house that had been lent to them temporarily by his family. My dad was now ready to get his own place. Actually, he already had one but couldn't move into it.

Two years before while living in Tomegbe, my dad had built a house in Agadji. It was a large place with four bedrooms. Actually, the house was not in Agadji; it was outside of the village about a mile from all the other houses, right in the middle of a cornfield. My father had decided to build out "in the jungle," so to speak, because that plot of land had been given to him following a long bitter dispute over sharing the family lands. It was that dispute that cost my parents the life of their first child. My dad's hope had been that building on the land would help him retain his claim to it until he and his family could return to Agadji. His hope was that by the time they were ready to move back, the village would have grown larger and come to include that area into the village property.

My father's plan had been a good one, but he was surprised by the course of events. His dear uncle's illness and death had forced my dad to come back to his village sooner than he had planned. Now he found himself in the position where he couldn't live in the prepared "farm" house with his family, especially with little ones.

When my father had first built the house, villagers who didn't like him very well made fun of him, saying he was "so crazy" that he built his first house "in the middle of a jungle." In fact, where my dad built the house was unusual, but as the years went by, that same house became very useful and is my family's present home.

As a result of these concerns, my dad decided to build a second house in the village. Right in front of the family's house that we were living in was a small, empty lot also owned by Father's family. After receiving authorization from the family, my father built this second house right in his home village among his relatives. This house had two bedrooms and an outside kitchen. When the house was completed, my father moved his family in.

During his first three years in Agadji, my father worked to jump-start his business as a tailor. Before long, people in Agadji were calling him Tailor, as he had been called in Tomegbe.

*****

When it came to clothes for their children, my mom and dad were and still are very, very fussy, perhaps because they both know a lot about sewing. Because they always wanted us to look very sharp, they were very picky when it came to choosing the quality of our shoes and the material our clothes were to be sewn from.

I remember watching my father sewing on his foot-powered Singer sewing machine day and night. I remember proudly wearing clothes sewn by my own dear father, Mr. Adade Koffi Edoh Otio Nicolas. He made our Catholic school uniforms—khaki shorts and white poplin shirts—for me and my dear older brother Fidel.

My older sister, Pauline and younger sister Jeanne, who was born later, had their clothes and school uniforms prepared by my mother, who also was a tailor. My mother, unlike my father, had handpowered Singer sewing machine.

As with many aspects of our culture, in Togo, men's and women's sewing machines are different—men's being powered with a foot pedal, women's with a handwheel. My parents both still have their machines today.

It wasn't until we were adolescents that my parents even allowed other tailors in our village or from those in Amlame or Atakpame to sew our clothes. My parents were especially picky about the tailors who would sew our clothes at special times of the year, such as Christmas, the New Year, and Easter.

I remember one of my parents' favorite male tailors in Agadji was Mr. Watara, a nice, well-built young guy from the Kotokoli tribe in the central region of Togo. He, like my dad, had learned to sew in Ghana. Mr. Watara had lived in Ghana for more than twenty years before moving to Agadji to be close to his parents and siblings, who had moved to Agadji years before from their home city of Sokode.

In my village, the quarter occupied by the Kotokoli ethnic group is called the Zongo. On every special occasion, my parents would have Mr. Watara make our clothes. Because Watara was very popular in my village, everybody wanted to have clothes made by him. Because Mr. Watara had lived for so many years in Ghana, he could not speak French, the official language of Togo, as could most people in Togo. Watara could not speak Akposso either. He was only fluent in his native Kotokoli and in English, neither of which was spoken by the average Agadji villager. He spoke some Ewe—one of the most popular native languages widely spoken in Togo and Ghana—which was also spoken as a second language by most people in my village. Because of these language barriers, it took longer as a family meeting than normal to explain one's desired outfit with its fashion and style to Mr. Watara, but once he had a clear picture of what a customer wanted, the job was always professionally done, and the results were always satisfactory.

Just watching Mr. Watara, anybody could tell he had just come from Ghana. In addition to his English, he dressed differently from people in my village. Also, his hair was always cut with beautiful lines in it. My father used to put these same kind of lines in my brother Fidel's hair and mine when we were little. Fidel and I were so crazy about that Ghanaian hairstyle that we would not go to church on Sundays without the lines in our hair.

Another of my parents' favorite tailors was Mr. Assim, like Mr. Watara, a man from the Kotokoli tribe; he lived in Amlame, a village near Agadji. Mr. Assim and Mr. Watara were the only tailors who could satisfy my parents' taste when it came to having clothes sewn for their boys. My father was also concerned and wanted to make sure that his own clothes would turn out beautiful, so he either sewed his own or also went to Mr. Watara or Mr. Assim.

As the years passed and styles changed, our parents turned to more professional tailors in big cities such as Atakpame, a city about twenty-eight miles from Agadji, where we went on two or three occasions to have our clothes made while we waited for village tailors like Watara and Assim to catch up with them.

*****

In my village, my dad's good reputation as a tailor didn't last long. He didn't stick to it long enough to become popular and attract more customers. In a sense, by working as a tailor, my dad tried to run away from his destiny. He tried to stay away from farming, but he was haunted by the profession of his ancestors. Now that he was back in Agadji, my dad's dilemma was whether to stay in tailoring and slowly lose control over his share of the family lands or to go back to his ancestors' profession of farming.

My father, as always, consulted with my mother about his decision. My mom was not only very supportive of my dad's idea but also decided to follow her husband in his new adventure—farming. Maybe this decision was easier for my parents because both had been born to and raised by farmers, so it might be said they had decided to return to their roots.

Maybe it's true that there is no place like home sweet home. Maybe it's true no one can teach an old dog new tricks. My parents, unlike an old dog, were born with these tricks in their blood; therefore, they could not escape them. My parents had been born farmers, had run away for a while, and like the Prodigal Son, one of the most beautiful stories in the Christian Bible, they decided to go back to their traditional activities.

Having made the decision to return to farming, my parents vowed not to sell their sewing machines but to save them in case one of their children decided to become a tailor. They also vowed to use their machines once in a while to keep their skills from getting rusty.

Finally rejecting the idea of pursuing both professions, my father finally hung the clean clothes of a tailor on the wall, put the dirty ones of a farmer on his back, and headed back to farming. In truth, my dad could not have lived with himself if he had failed to work the farmlands that he had won only after bitter family fights that had had very painful consequences—they had cost him the life of at least one child and could have even cost him his own life.

As they had both grown up as farmers, my parents' adjustment to the profession was smooth. Even in Ghana, during his tailor apprenticeship, my father had had to interrupt his training and work on farms to earn money.

As a farmer, my father got up as early as five in the morning. He always got up at the second cry of the rooster, and by sunrise, he was already where he wanted to be. About 90 percent of the time, he was on his farm before we got up, around six. As he always said, the most productive time for a farmer is before sunrise.

Growing up, I don't remember seeing my father around the house in the morning. The only time we would see him in the morning was when he had other places to go beside the farm or when he had to take care of some domestic business, such as a family meeting.

Not only was my father an early bird, he ate like one too. After he got up, he usually ate from leftovers from dinner the night before, packed something for lunch, and then hit the road. Unlike most farmers and other hard workers who eat a lot to compensate for the energy they put out, my father can exist with only a handful of rice for breakfast. Sometimes, all he ate during lunch was a piece of fruit, papaya, pineapple, avocado, or mango—all of which came from his farms.

Other than a small lunch, the only thing my father took with him to the fields was his jug of water. Whatever the time of year—the rainy season when creeks were overflowing or the dry season when drinkable water was scarce because the creeks had dried up—he had to have his jug of water.

My dad, no doubt, had developed these eating habits during his painful childhood and continued them during his apprenticeship time in Ghana. Maybe that's why my father has the smallest build in his family. He only weighs about 110 pounds and is only about five feet and two inches tall, but he is a very tough cookie and very resilient.

*****

My father worked hard and long hours. As a result, we children often did not see him but we did become acquainted with his work. On Saturdays, since we didn't have school, my father would get up fairly late (for him), so we could go with him to the farm.

Otherwise, we would not see him all day until he returned home from his farms at seven at night or later. He was very dedicated.

As kids, we had the privilege of spending an entire day in a week with our daddy at home, and it was on Sundays. In that regard, my father was loyal to his Catholic faith.

He has never done any farmwork on Sundays.

Our family ritual for Sunday actually began on Saturday night after dinner. At that time, my dad would make sure our Sunday outfits were ironed and ready for mass. In the morning, he always made sure the lines in our hair were straight before we went to church; actually, Fidel and I wouldn't have let him forget.

Every Sunday, my father took my older brother Fidel and me to church. Our older sister Pauline went with Mom. At church, we enjoyed listening to him say prayers and sing songs in Latin. Like most villagers, he did this without knowing the first letter of the Latin alphabet. I'm tempted to swear my dad had the best voice in the village. Perhaps I gathered this impression because we only hear him sing once a week. Whether it is a fair appraisal really isn't important. After all, don't many children think that way about their parents, their role models, their stars? Don't we all think that our mom cooks the best sauce? Oh well, allow me my childhood prejudices.

*****

Not long after my parents decided to become farmers, my younger sister, my last sibling, Jeanne, was born. Jeanne, like all of us, was born healthy. Dedicated as my parents were to protecting their children, Jeanne never had to deal with mysterious illnesses or problems. Her birth brought another special joy to my family. My parents always wanted to have a well-balanced family, and thanks to the good Lord, they ended up with just that: two boys, Fidel and Pierre, and two girls, Pauline and Jeanne.

I was only about two when Jeanne was born. I don't remember much what happened that day, only that as a two-year-old, I wasn't very happy to see Jeanne because she stole my mom away from me. I was afraid that all the special attention I was used to getting from my mom would be gone because of this new baby. I was furious, I was jealous, but in the end, I was also happy because everybody around me was very happy, and more importantly, my dear mother didn't treat me differently, at least not right away. It was crystal clear to me that my parents still loved me, too, so why be unhappy? Still, I couldn't help being somewhat jealous.

*****

Even though coffee and cocoa are the two major crops grown in the plateau region where my village is, as a beginner farmer, my dad started with regular farming—that is, growing corn, peanuts, beans, and other local crops unknown to the West, such as fonio. One of my father's first farms was located about a mile from the village on the same land as his "jungle" house.

When my brother, sisters, and I accompanied my father to the farm, it was not like work but like entering another, more magical world. We chased lizards and played hide-and-seek and other games. I remember it being surrounded by beautiful dark green corn and peanut leaves.

*****

Though we children were adjusting quite well to our new environment, there were things about life in the village that we missed. I personally missed those beautiful full moon nights when friends of my age group and a little older got together under a big mango tree located behind our kitchen. There we took turn telling folk tales. I will never forget a favorite folk tale of mine about Turtle that goes as follow:

Turtle and birds used to be very good friends. One year, in the village where they were living, there was a severe drought. The drought was so harsh that some inhabitants were near starvation. It was during that time of misery that birds and Turtle received an invitation to a dinner party at God's house.

Because God's house was located in the sky somewhere in the clouds, it was obvious to Turtle that he could not attend the dinner because he did not have wings and could not fly. Turtle was convinced that unless he came up with a solution to his situation, he might starve to death. Turtle then called up his bird-friends and declared: "I would love to go to the dinner party, but as you all know, I'm unable to fly. I, therefore, need you guys to help me out, or I will not make it."

"How can we help you, dear friend?" one of the birds replied.

Turtle paused for a moment and continued, "Well, if each one of you would let me borrow one or couple of your feathers, I can make me two artificial wings that will allow me to fly like you guys... please." After consultation among themselves, the birds agreed to let their dear friend Turtle borrow a few of their feather so he also could attend the dinner party.

The day of the party arrived, and the birds were most excited to see their friend Turtle with his beautiful new multicolored wings, ready to join them at this very special event. In the middle of all the excitement, Turtle was secretly designing a vicious plan.

A few minutes prior to their departure, Turtle called the birds together one more time and suggested that they picked individual names in order to help avoid confusion at the party and in case their host, God, would want to call them by their names. Once again, the birds agreed with Turtle and picked names. When came time for Turtle to pick his own, he decided that he would be called "all of you."

At the party, there were a lot of people. Shortly after their arrival, one of God's servant brought on a big dish full of food. As the servant was getting ready to leave, Turtle asked him, "E-e-excuse me, sir, who is this food for?"

Without hesitation, the servant replied, "All of you." Turtle then happily turned to his friends and declared, "Did you hear that? This is my food, yours will be coming up next."

Turtle, hungry as he was, started eating the food all by himself while his friends anxiously waited for their meal to come. Disappointed that their food was taking so long to come, the birds decided to return home. Turtle went with them, but unlike his poor friends, he was delighted that his little trick had worked.

A second invitation came to Turtle and his bird friends, and again Turtle pulled the same trick and got away with it. Then a third invitation came, but this time, Turtle was not so lucky. The servant brought the food, and Turtle claimed it as his, so he filled his stomach while his bird friends again went hungry. However, the birds finally got furious at their so-called friend for being greedy and decided to teach him a lesson. Before returning home for a third time with empty stomachs, they decided to take their feathers back from Turtle. Before Turtle had a chance to talk the birds into reconsidering, they stripped him of their wings. The last bird was about to leave when Turtle, now very powerless, asked him for one last favor.

"Hey, my friend," Turtle called to the last bird, "I understand that you are all mad at me and I am terribly sorry, but I just want you to do me one last favor, would you?"

"What favor?" the last bird replied angrily.

"Well," Turtle continued, "now that I have lost my wings, as you can see, I can't fly. I have no choice but to jump home from up here, so if you wouldn't mind, upon your return to earth, please go to my house and take all the pillows and soft blankets and place them in front of my porch so that when I jump, I can land on them and not hurt myself. Would you please do that little favor for me?" Turtle pleaded.

"I will do just that," the last bird replied and flew off.

When the last bird arrived on earth, she told the other birds about the favor she was going to do for Turtle. However, instead of doing as Turtle asked, the birds worked together to fill the area in front of his porch with hard items—rocks, stones, dry wood, any hard item that they could think of that would hurt Turtle instead of giving him a smooth landing.

Turtle took one last deep breath and jumped from up above. His landing taught him a tough lesson. His body was badly broken into small pieces. After months of intensive care, a local traditional medicine man managed to save Turtle's life, but he would forever remain deformed, unable to walk as fast as he used to and with short legs, a neck that stuck out, and a body that carried the scars where all the broken pieces had been sewn back together. So was created the new look of Turtle that we all know today.

*****

As the years went by, my father began to show interest in growing coffee and cocoa, waiting to gain experience in the field as a farmer before taking on a different kind of farming. Compared with growing cereal grains, growing coffee and cocoa is more demanding. It requires a lot of patience, strength, and guts.

In mountainous regions like mine, the vegetation is 80 percent deep forest, which contains the best soil for cocoa and coffee. To grow these crops requires cutting down the biggest trees in the area so that the ground can be exposed to the sun's rays that the plants need to grow. As we all know, without sunlight, a plant will not generate needed chlorophyll. Therefore, at least 40 percent of trees with many leaves and those that are very tall are cut down or their branches are trimmed off. This first phase of preparing the farm can take weeks, depending on the size of the farm. All work is done by hand.

Next, the felled trees are cut into smaller pieces. The women carry about 98 percent of the branches home to use as firewood. The remaining debris is put in small piles around the farm and burned. This practice, known as the "slash and burn" technique, has good and bad points. On the good side, it helps farmers get the job done quickly; the bad part is that by burning branches on the ground, some bacteria that make the soil fertile is killed, leaving the soil with less nutrients. Another potential danger exists in that too often these well-intentioned fires get out of hand, become wildfires, and destroy farms. Preventive measures are always taken, but because these activities usually take place prior to the rainy season when conditions are driest, things can and do get out of hand.

Most often the clearing of farms is completed before June, which marks the beginning of the rainy season. A few days after the burnings, the farmers start digging holes in which the young coffee or cocoa plants will be planted.

These young plants are transported from their seedbeds, located on the banks of the river or creek nearest the farms. These plants are about nine inches tall: they will be well taken care of and protected (almost the way good mothers care for their newborns) until they are old enough to start producing.

My father was well aware of the hard work and other details of growing cocoa and coffee. Remember, before he went to Ghana to become a tailor, he had worked on his uncle's coffee and cocoa farms, some of which he inherited.

*****

Just as my father was ready to work hard to support himself and his family, he was also willing to help others. My father would literally give someone who needed it the shirt off his back, but he is also very opinionated. My dad listened and was always eager to learn from others; he could also be very stubborn. He lived and played by the rules and expected others to do the same. He apologized when he was wrong and spoke his mind, fought for his rights and survival, and defended the weak who were being cheated and bullied. My father always tried to do things right.

My dad's moral qualities, in addition to his hard work, very quickly made him one of the most respected, feared, and admired men in my village, Agadji, as well as in Amlame and the surrounding villages.

My father doesn't know how to go out and socialize—maybe he doesn't have to, but he is the best host any stranger or foreigner could ever meet. He and my mother both know how to make a stranger feel safe and at home.

The only social activity that I can recall my dad being associated with was soccer. He was a very good amateur soccer player when he was young, and he stopped playing only after a head injury, which still makes him cough frequently. Because of his impressive skill, he was named president of my village's soccer team during the early '70s. I remember those good old days following the victories of the team. For a very long time, under my dad's leadership, the soccer team in my village was the most feared in the region.

After a game, the whole village would come to our house straight from the soccer field. As a kid, I used to love to see the whole village pouring into our home. It made me feel like a little prince. Everyone would be singing beautiful glorious songs, one of which was a favorite. I still love this French song.

> Jouer au ballon c'est agréable
> Jouer au ballon c'est bon
> Mais il ne faut pas jouer avec égoïsme
> Jouer au ballon c'est agréable
> Jouer au ballon c'est bon."

The translation follows:

> Playing soccer is fun
> playing soccer is good
> But don't you play with an ego
> Playing soccer is fun
> Playing soccer is good.

The soccer team came to our house not only to show appreciation for my dad's leadership but also to have drinks and refreshments and to hold their final meeting before going home. The meeting always followed a game whether the team won or lost.

*****

Not everybody in my dad's family appreciated his fast-growing respect and reputation. While some were applauding my dad, others spent their time being jealous or looking for ways to hurt or eliminate my father. My dad was very aware of all this but was by no means frightened.

After a while, my dad became used to being hated by his enemies. He even enjoyed confronting and fighting them. My father came to realize that after each disagreement with his enemies (and he had quite a few), he learned something new; in addition, these enemies made themselves known, giving my father a chance to know whom he should be friends with and whom he should deal with more carefully.

My father's situation is like that of a frog whose enemies thought that throwing him in a river would be the best way to punish or get rid of him. Frogs love water; therefore, throwing him in the river is like sending him to paradise. What else can the frog say to his enemies, but "Thank you very, very much!"

Yes. My father, like the frog, knew to thank his enemies. In fact, as his personal way of sending a clear message to his enemies, my father wrote above the two main entrances to his house in the village two statements: "Thank God" and "Thanks to my enemies."

My father has always thought that in the end, it was not bad to have enemies because by pushing him around or chasing him, the enemies made him find new ways to survive and, therefore, new ways to protect himself and, above all, his family.

*****

In 1971 to 1972, the French Catholic priests in my village requested more land to add classrooms to the Catholic primary school. A special, secret meeting was held among the elders of the village. One decision from that meeting was to respond positively and quickly to the priest's request. In addition, some elders, my dad's enemies, suggested giving the priests more land than they had asked for. They suggested giving away two-fifths of my dad's "jungle" farmland to the priests—the same land on which my father had built his first house. As soon as my father became aware of this situation, he became very angry. These people made my father's reaction to the matter worse by claiming the land was community property and denying my father's ownership of the land.

This action caused my father to declare war on his enemies. My father, for the very first time, broke away from tradition, which required land disputes to be handled by the village chief; instead, my dad took his case directly to court. There he was victorious; two-thirds of the villagers were behind my dad, only one-third against him.

I vividly remember that Tuesday early in the afternoon when my dad's supporters brought him home. He was covered with white baby bath powder—white being a symbol of peace, victory, and joy in my Akposso tribe. Yes, my dad had won the battle in court.

As we children grew, our two-bedroom house seemed to become smaller. My father started thinking about moving his family to his first house, a mile from the center of the village and still far from the edges of the village—as I have said, in the middle of the jungle.

As always, my father made my mom aware of his plan. My mom resisted the idea of raising her family in the jungle, far from friends and too close, as she saw it, to wild animals. My mother also didn't like the idea of leaving her female friends, but at the same time, she, like my father, was ready to make any sacrifice for the well-being of her children. Slowly but surely, my mother digested the idea until she made up her mind and told my father she was ready to move.

My parents also wanted to move to put an end to the many small disputes they were having with neighbors and family members. My parents were convinced that if their own people couldn't set aside their jealousies, then they would prefer to live at peace in the "jungle," listening to the beautiful songs of birds every day. Separating from these people would be worth it—in fact, it would be enjoyable.

A few days after they decided to move, my dad sped up the remodeling of our new home, and within two weeks in the summer of 1972 to 1973, we moved and ceased to be part of the village. My dad gave a special name to our new home to symbolize his hopes for our life there. He called it Megbeadzre, which in Ewe means "I don't want any trouble or stories" or simply "Peace."

At our new home, life was very different. We children temporarily lost the companionship of our best friends.

Also, life, especially during the first two years, was more dangerous than it had been in the village. We lived and fought with reptiles, especially snakes. Snakes were attracted to the eggs our chickens laid, and at night, they found it hard to resist the heat from our lanterns and kitchen. They found the latter especially attractive during the rainy season, for when it's cold, reptiles are constantly looking for warm places to hide.

Still, life was fun. We children adapted our games to our new environment, our new life. Instead of playing hideand-seek in and around houses as when we were living in the village, the compound trees provided us with hiding places. We also learned to use parts of trees as our toys, like using branches and leaves to build houses that only lasted until a strong wind swept through the compound.

As a family, we stuck together, protecting each other from our common enemies, whether they came from the jungle (the snakes, scorpions, and reptiles) or from the village (the witches, wizards, and jealous people).

Not long after we moved to our new home, the Catholic priests' project to expand their school became a reality. The elementary school was moved from the priests' compound and set up only a few yards from our new home. This was good news, especially to us children! Not only didn't we have to walk half a mile to school like before, but we also were able to make new friends, many more friends, indeed.

With the school closer to us, more houses sprung up around us. Before we knew it, the former jungle had become part of the village under the name of Megbeadzre or Peace—the same name my father had given to our home, the very first house built in that area. Looking back, I think my father was right to have thanked his enemies, for if it hadn't been for them, my dad wouldn't have thought about leaving the village. Thanks to his enemies, my father's name has gone down in the history of our village as the founder of the well-known residential area of Megbeadzre. And as my father likes to say, thanks above all to the Almighty Good Lord through whom everything comes about.

My dad and the whole family was beginning to look at life differently, more positively, and for good reasons. We left the village, but now the village was coming to us. We were becoming an incredibly happy family.

Perhaps it was this positive feeling that led my father to finally decide in 1974 to become a coffee grower. That year, the Togo government introduced new varieties of coffee and cocoa plants. The varieties would not require less work from the farmers but would mature faster and would produce more beans. These new plants had been tested in laboratories and were shown to start producing in two to three years. The varieties that had been introduced to the west coast of Africa in the nineteenth century by German and English colonizers matured in six to eight years.

In 1974, the government of Togo began organizing villages in my coffee and cocoa region; there were many campaigns where farmers were introduced to these new plant varieties, especially coffee. At first, the government received a very cool reaction from the farmers. While some were willing to give these new plants a shot, the more conservative ones turned their backs. The negative attitude of these farmers was understandable. Even if their existing coffee plants were old and ready to be replaced, they were still producing and providing income for their families. Why take a risk now?

Abandoning their "old-style" coffee farms in the name of progress and switching to these new plant varieties would create financial hardship, and the farmers were convinced there was no guarantee the new varieties would really be better. These farmers were afraid of the unknown; it can be to break old habits.

My dad, who had never let himself be dominated by fear, decided to try the new coffee varieties. My dad's fear may have been minimized by the simple fact that he was a newcomer to the coffee business; therefore, he knew he really had nothing to lose and he might have something to gain if the project turned out well.

After making his own decision, my father then went out and convinced a young close cousin to join him in growing the new coffee. My dad's cousin used a close friendship with the Catholic priests to borrow an acre of their land for an experimental coffee farm. Without hesitation, the priests lent them the land, which was halfway between their "mission" and the new Catholic school compound and next to our home at Megbeadzre.

The agreement between my dad and his cousin was to join efforts to raise the coffee and afterward split the farm between them. They would challenge each other to put their best personal effort forward to see who could obtain the better harvest on his portion of the farm.

While the land and coffee were free, thanks to the priests and the government, my father and his cousin had to buy fertilizer (which did not come cheap) from the government to help the coffee grow faster and stronger. The fertilizer in a forty-pound nylon bag cost about $1 each, and the amount required depended on the size of the farm. My father would later spend about fifty dollars on fertilizer to treat all his farms.

My father, highly motivated as always, didn't wait to reap his first harvest from his experimental farm before he took a commanding lead in this new generation of coffee plant project. Four or six months after the first coffee was planted on the priests' property, my father signed up to grow more, this time on a bigger farm, which was his own land. He carefully followed all the needed steps. He cut down the coffee plants on two of his old coffee farms that he had inherited from relatives and started planting the new coffee.

Only two or three farmers in my village followed in my dad's footsteps that year, and one became my dad's companion in this new endeavor', eventually replacing his cousin. This farmer, a very good friend of my father, was Mr. Kabine, who was as tough-minded, devoted to farming, and hardworking as my dad.

Mr. Kabine and my dad greatly enjoyed each other's company and mutually respected each other. Even though Mr. Kabine was an immigrant from Atakpame, twenty miles from Agadji, my father dealt with him fairly and treated him like a native of our village and as a good friend. Mr. Kabine was one of the very few close friends of my father's that I can remember. While their friendship was only work-oriented, due to the fact that my father was not the kind of person who would socialize just for the sake of doing so, it was very strong, and they were excellent coworkers.

Each morning after breakfast, Mr. Kabine and my father would meet at our house or his, depending on whose farm they were going to on a particular day.

My father and Mr. Kabine's farms were five good miles apart, and both farms showed such good results—producing healthy plants with abundant coffee beans—that soon other farmers began following in their footsteps, planting the new coffee and seeking advice from them.

While Mr. Kabine focused his efforts on his 1975 farm, my dad was busy expanding his farms each year. My father's influence spread far beyond my village for whom he quickly became a role model. They rediscovered his resolve to do things right as well as becoming the advisor and organizer of everybody else who decided to begin growing the new SRCC coffee.

My father, as an eager student will do, listened to advice from and followed all the steps required by the SRCC, the government's Coffee and Cocoa Renovation Society. Due to my father's hard work and determination from day one, he was soon recognized by the SRCC as their best coffee-growing client and he quickly became a good personal friend of the government-appointed Director of the SRCC agency's regional headquarters in Agadji, Mr. Gadzaro.

His fellow farmers recognized him as the best when it came to listening to and implementing recommendations from SRCC officials, and everybody knew it.

As a new farmer and just because he had always been used to hard work, my father never rested. Maybe he never learned how to rest when he was little. My dear father enjoyed, no, loved working hard and long hours—twelve to fourteen hours a day, Monday through Sunday, if necessary. I've never seen my father sitting at home all day long simply because he didn't feel like working or going to his farms that day. Never. Perhaps there was an occasional Sunday when he didn't work, but it wasn't because he didn't enjoy farming. My father went to his farms every day no matter what. Even when he didn't feel very well, he went and did what he called "easy work."

When my dad was not on his own farms working all day, he was at home fulfilling his role as head of the family; he was a good husband and a good father. He was never seen wasting his time socializing in the village, even though he was friendly to everyone.

Because my father was so involved in planting the new coffee varieties and so well respected, most coffee growers in my village and the government used our home as a distribution center for the young coffee plants and for tons of fertilizers. From our home, the supplies were transported to the farms.

A few days before the arrival of the coffee plants, my father's excitement infected all of us. At that time, my father, with the help of my brother Fidel and myself, began to prepare a temporary storage area for the soon-to-arrive young coffee plants.

The chosen storage place was under the huge mango tree that stood a few meters from my mother's little mud kitchen. This mango tree was an ideal place because of the huge area that its wide, leafy branches shaded. Because this mango tree was at the edge of our compound and very close to the wild grass, my father made sure that we cleared and weeded it before the plants arrived.

If the weather was hot and there had not been rain in a while, my father ordered us to wet down the area both to keep the dust down and to provide some freshness from the ground to the plants.

Not until the preparations were done would my father relax a little while waiting for the coffee truck to pull into his compound. When the truck did arrive, everyone jumped into action.

I still remember one Saturday morning in 1975, my three siblings—Pauline, Fidel, Jeanne—and myself were helping our father and a dozen relatives unload two big yellow government trucks of young coffee plants at our Megbeadzre home. These trucks had four, five, or more trips to make each day to supply farmers with plants, so we had to unload our plants as quickly as possible.

These plants weighed about five pounds each because they came in black plastic bags filled with good dirt to help maintain the plants during transportation until they were planted. The truck unloading was performed much the way an assembly line works in a factory with each worker having a specific task. To begin, three or four men got in the truck. The first man carefully picked up a coffee plant and passed it to the next man and on to the next until it reached the end of the truck and was handed to the first person standing on the ground. That first person on the ground played the most important role; the man or woman had to be extra careful so that the young, fragile coffee plant would not drop to the ground. This person passed the plant safely onto the next and to the next in the line of six or seven people until the plants finally reached the last person who carefully set it on the ground, in a storage area open to the sky.

That last person in the line was my father. He chose that position to make sure that each coffee plant arrived safely in the storage area and to sort and organize the plants. My father carefully separated the healthy-looking plants from the sickly ones, which he immediately gave intensive care; he did not want to waste or lose one of these precious coffee plants. As soon as the truck was unloaded, my father watered any sickly-plants. If he happened to have fertilizer handy, he would feed them small quantities, just enough to give these poor plants some badly needed strength.

After the final delivery of coffee plants between my dad and Mr. Kabine, my dad paid the Catholic school to have the elder students help transport them to his farm on the slope of the mountain about a mile from our house and the school compound. This activity was beneficial to both my father and the school. My dad benefited because with the help of transporting the plants, he could focus more on getting them planted. The Catholic school benefited because each year it worked to raise money that it used for special activities, including a dinner party that was held at the end of the school year before everyone left on vacation.

*****

That year, the weather was kind to my father and the other farmers. The rains came on time, and the shining sun helped the plants to create the chlorophyll they needed. The coffee plants looked healthy with their dark green leaves. My dad was so pleased with the results he was getting on his coffee farms and with his fast-growing reputation as one of the best coffee growers that he didn't hesitate to sign his second farm up for the project the following year.

My father named his farms by the year he began raising coffee on them. The first was 1975, which was a small farm, only about one acre. Then came 1976 and 1977, which really were extensions of 1975 on the same acreage.

In 1976, my father was unanimously voted president and chairman of the Coffee Growers Association in my region. In fact, for five consecutive years, from 1976 to 1982, my dad was president of the coffee growers. As president, my father solved or helped solve problems among his fellow coffee growers. He organized meetings at SRCC headquarters or at our home to discuss work-related issues. He reminded the farmers of upcoming activities, such as signing up for or picking up new plants or fertilizers. He also gave farmers advice based on his own experience. My father hated being in debt, so when it came to making payments to SRCC for fertilizer loans, fees, or others bills, my dad was very conscientious—another characteristic which made him a good president.

Within four years of planting his first coffee farm, my father had become the most respected coffee grower in the region. He received the highest respect from SRCC top officials, especially Mr. Gadzaro, his replacement Mr. M'PO, and Mr. Jill Akitani, the first accountant of SRCC.

In 1978, 1979, and 1980, my father and other good workers, among them Mr. Kabine, were chosen by the SRCC office in Agadji to attend the regional fair in Atakpame as well as the national fair in the capital city of Lome. At the national fair, all the participants, including my father and Mr. Kabine, received a modest but significant award from the President of State, Gen. Gnassimgbe Eyadema.

*****

Growing coffee has always kept my father very busy all year round, that is why he has always been a happy man. He would probably go crazy if he ever had nothing to do. To give an idea of just how busy my dad was, I would like to describe the types of work he did during the farming year.

During April (which marked the end of one coffee season), my dad spent three to six weeks helping my mother with her home farm activities. Together they harvested cereal grains from the family gardens and prepared the fields for the next planting. He also worked on small repairs around the compound, including remodeling work, building new silos and repairing old ones, and repairing tools.

Toward the end of May or the beginning of June, before the first rain touched the ground, my dad, with the help of all our family, would begin the cycle of caring for the coffee plants. My father was a careful farmer and not about to risk harming his coffee plants, so he always kept his eyes trained on us when we were working with him on his farms. I think it's fair to say that when it comes to working on his farms, my dad does not trust anybody but himself, not even his honey—my mother.

If new coffee plants were going to be put in, then prior to their arrival, my dad, with the help of my mother and us children, prepared the farms. We cleared them of the big trees that gave too much shade, burned the small branches, piled up larger branches to be taken home and used as firewood, and dug small holes throughout the farm. The holes were carefully laid out in a crisscross pattern. They were two to three meters apart so that air would be able to circulate between the mature plants. We did this work together as a family united in sweat and laughter.

Then there were always the existing plants to care for. For them, the first task scheduled on the farming year was fertilizing. On my father's farms, fertilizer had to be applied with great care to each plant; it was a law!

The fertilizer was of two kinds: one helped the coffee plants grow well, and the other helped them produce as many coffee beans as possible. The difference was important.

During the school year, we children helped my father on his farms as much as possible after school and all day Saturday. Whenever Pauline, Fidel, myself, and Jeanne didn't have school, early in the morning, we four would each take two or three bags full of fertilizer to the farm, well wrapped in nice plastic covers to protect it from rain or water. Because the fertilizers were mixed on the farm in large pans and poured into small buckets that we carried from one plant to the next and because we could be easily confused about which fertilizer to use on which plant, my father required us to fertilize the plants one row at a time.

In addition, my father, fussy as he always was, made sure we used the proper amount and strength of fertilizer as required by the SRCC, so he watched us closely as we applied the fertilizer, pouring it around each plant. We had to be careful to give each plant the correct dosage. For the one- and two-year-old plants, we'd only use a half-dose per plant. The three-year-old plants were old enough to handle the full measurement of fertilizer. The measuring cup we used, and which was required by the SRCC, was two-thirds the size of an American beer can for the adult coffee plants.

My father's rules also controlled how we were to apply the fertilizer. First, we had to push aside the dead leaves lying on the ground around the coffee plants, draw a circle around each plant, spray the fertilizer inside the circle in a circular motion, and finally cover the fertilizer with the same dead leaves.

These steps were essential to help the fertilizer dissolve and to prevent rain from washing it away. Also, the SRCC people had told my father that if the fertilizer was too close to the plants, the strong chemicals could do serious harm, so he would not tolerate the fertilizer any closer to the plants than they had said. My dad didn't have to have a PhD in chemistry to heed the warnings of the SRCC people; the possibility of harming his coffee plants that he and his family were working so hard to grow was enough to keep him careful.

Depending on the size of the farm and the weather, fertilizing could continue for weeks. The only breaks in the work happened when it rained. Fertilizer couldn't be applied in the rain because it would melt away quickly.

*****

Over the years, my dad developed a self-imposed discipline or work ethic that contributed to his reputation as a good farmer. He would often tackle one or two minor tasks while working on a major one.

For instance, while fertilizing, my father always took a couple of seconds to weed around the coffee plants and to remove any dead branches he saw. Even though weeding and trimming each had a set time and place on the farming schedule, my dad felt that allowing himself to deviate from his main task and attend to other small tasks at the same time allowed him to cut the time spent on each individual item on his list by at least 20 percent. When others asked if maybe he was being disorganized, my father always replied that by taking a few extra moments and being careful in his tasks, he saved time in the long run and kept the farm nice and clean all the time.

Even though I understand my father's motives, I was one of his biggest critics at the time. I was the person in my family who hated farm activities the most, and I used to go nuts whenever my father would ask me to try and attend to more than one task at a time. In truth, if I had had a choice, I wouldn't have done even the one that was on the schedule.

*****

My dad knew fertilizing had to be completed before the rainy season began, so of course, this was his top priority. He would complete his work by finding excuses to work very late on his farms.

My mom was very proud of how dedicated my dad was to his work. Still, she worried about him when he was gone long after dark. One day, it got to eight at night. It was very dark out, and my dear father still hadn't shown up at home.

My mom went looking for him, and when she could not find my father, she became scared. She was scared of losing my father, scared of raising four young children alone, scared of what might happen to her and the kids if he suddenly disappeared from our lives. In fact, she was so scared that she cried her eyes out.

When my father finally returned home and found my mother in tears, he promised never to stay that late on his farms again. Unfortunately, that good promise did not last long. My dad kept coming home late from his farm. Eventually, he ran out of excuses as to why he was breaking his promise, and my poor mom decided she had no choice but to get used to his habits.

My dear father, today in his early sixties, still returns home very late from his farms every day.

*****

Because of the number of farms my dad had and the time limits that nature imposes, sometimes he couldn't get a particular job done with only himself and our family helping before the rains came. In these rare cases, my dad would hire help—good part-time farmers.

My dad has always been a happy man. What has really made him so happy was not the attention he received wherever he went, but he simply loved being a coffee grower and a good farmer. Like good farmers everywhere, my father constantly watched the sky and prayed for good weather. Too often, the sky surprises farmers. They rarely get what they expect, or if they do, there is either not enough or too much of it. It either rains too much without enough sun or there's too much sun with too little rain or it's too windy and so on.

The sky makes farmers look bad; it makes them look like they are greedy, never satisfied with what they get. It unfairly makes them look like they always have something to complain about.

In reality, when weather conditions are perfect, there are no happier or more satisfied people on earth as farmers. They enjoy themselves by taking advantage of the good days, working late and extra hard on those days because of the uncertainty of tomorrow's weather, the unreliable nature of the sky. Their greatest happiness is to see their crops grow beautifully. The happiness and satisfaction they feel just before a successful harvest, looking out over their fine, healthy plants, is like that parents feel when they watch their children grow up healthy, succeeding in what they are doing.

Unfortunately, days of perfect weather occur few and far between, and good farmers lose a lot of sleep, worrying about their poor farms. As a result, good farmers like my own dad actually enjoy "abusing" their bodies by working overtime on the farms whenever they can. At those times, they pay little attention to their wives' worries.

*****

Shortly after the fertilizing was completed, anywhere from mid-June to mid-July, my father would tackle his next major project on the farm calendar—weeding. Weeding activities are heaviest during our three-month long school recess, which begins at the end of June.

While women do demanding work, such as transporting massive amounts of firewood to the homes from the forests and farms, weeding is considered inappropriate and too dangerous for them;

only men do it. In our family, my dad, Fidel, and I did the weeding, while my mom, my older sister Pauline, and my younger sister Jeanne worked at their domestic tasks, such as doing dishes and the laundry.

Around six in the morning, after a breakfast of leftovers, my father, my older brother Fidel, and myself would sharpen our coupe-coupe or machete, the only tool appropriate for weeding on coffee and cocoa farms.

Sharpening a coupe-coupe is a skill taught to young boys by their elders—fathers or older brothers. Great attention is given to grinding both sides of the same edge of the 'coupecoupe with tremendous energy and accuracy against a special rock, adding cold water to minimize the friction, until the tool is razor sharp.

Once done sharpening our tools, we three men would head to the farm. As soon as we arrived, especially when we were working with our dad, we immediately went to work. We would work until sunset with only one break when the women showed up with our lunch.

My father loved to work with his two sons. My father enjoyed this not only because of the help he was getting from us but more importantly because it was his golden opportunity to instruct us on the art—rather, his art—of farming. I also believe he liked to seize the opportunity to show off a little by beating my brother Fidel and I in many ways—accuracy, speed, technique—as if to say "Aha! Got ya. Even if you can beat me with what you learn in school, I can beat you, including your teachers, on my farms."

Another reason he loved to work with his sons was, it provided him with one of the few occasions besides when we sat down to eat that he could talk about men's issues, and my father loved to talk. He also took these opportunities to show us the limits of his farms and to introduce us to whomever he shared a farm with.

Weeding basically consists of cutting weeds as short as possible, preferably close to their roots, with the very sharp coupe-coupe. One must hold the coupe-coupe flat, parallel to the ground, sort of the way a batter swings at the ball in American baseball. The coupe-coupe is swung with great energy and force across the body. The upper body moves toward the weeds or other object being cut down, and the feet are kept way back. This results in the body curving in an arch. This position helps the user to avoid or minimize injuries because accidents do occur, and when they do, they are nasty.

Often those injuries occur when the feet are in the wrong position or when the coupe-coupe slips out of the user's hands because he isn't holding on tight enough. For the most part, these accidents lead the recipient to the hospital. In 95 percent of the cases, legs are hurt during these accidents. These injuries are the reason men do this work.

As we were weeding, my father made sure we put a thick layer of cut weeds under each plant to prevent the hot sun from burning the roots of his plants and to preserve the moisture in the soil. My dad always made sure all the little, important details were done right.

The exact amount of time need to complete the weeding varied depending on the number and size of the farms as well as the number of the people helping; it often took weeks.

In addition to the children working, especially during summer recess, villagers got help from relatives or organized themselves into small teams and took turns working on each other's farms, in the kind of arrangement my dad and his colleague Mr. Kabine had. Helping one another with the farmwork is another example of the very strong sense of community life in my village; everybody watches out for everybody, everybody helps everybody out. It is a nice thing to do and a lovely way to live together! One way or another, the farmwork got done on time.

Almost immediately, when the weeding was done, my father began another task, one that most coffee growers neglect. He examined each coffee plant and cut off any extra new branches developing next to the three or four main branches recommended by the SRCC. The idea was not to let a coffee plant become overburdened with too many branches. Too many branches would reduce the productivity of the plants.

New branches usually appeared during the rainy season, after the plants were fertilized, so my dad always waited until he was done fertilizing and weeding before tackling this project.

Around the end of August or the beginning of September, the coffee plants would develop wonderfully scented white flowers, which announced the coming of the coffee pods. Having completed the inspection of his plants, my dad would temporarily stay away from his farms so as not to disturb the growth of those very sensitive flowers and, thereby, the coffee bean crop.

During that time, my father cleaned his silos and areas where the harvested coffee pods would be dried. Depending on the likely productivity of his farms in a particular year, he might also build new silos.

Harvest season starts late October or early November and has always been the farmer's busiest time of the year. My father had so many acres of coffee that he no longer tried to harvest the coffee with only himself and his family. He put my mother in charge of hiring people from our village and the surrounding small farms to help harvest. My mother took her jobs as seriously as my father and planned in advance, so she always completed the hiring two to three weeks before the harvest season actually started. It usually required fifteen to twenty people, most of whom were good women workers.

These workers were paid based on the quantity of pods harvested, so there was always a sense of competition among them. Some would go to my dad's farms before others to have the chance to harvest more. All went to the farms as early as they could and harvested all day long. As they worked, the women made the task more enjoyable by telling jokes, gossiping, or singing.

My mom would always bring the workers lunch at midday. She would bring the meal out to the farms so they would not have to stop working for long.

At the end of the day, my mom, sometimes assisted by my dad, measured the quantity harvested by each employee and paid them accordingly. Once the coffee pods had been measured, those same good ladies sometimes helped transport the pods to our Megbeadzre home to be dried.

The coffee pods started out a dark green and then turned yellow and finally red when it was time to harvest. Coffee pods harvested prematurely (especially when green) had to be thrown away.

Because of that, my father worked to make sure that no green coffee pods were harvested; the yellow ones are acceptable because they are almost ready, but never the green pods, not on my dad's farms.

Every evening, upon returning home from school at around 5:30 p.m. during the harvest, my siblings and I went to the coffee farms and helped transport the harvested pods home to be dried. We enjoyed doing the work as part of our contribution to our dad's effort. After all, he was there for us whenever we needed him. At times when we were overwhelmed by the huge quantity of the coffee pods waiting to be transported home, in addition to the ladies working for us, my parents would ask close relatives to come and give us a hand. Because our home was located on the edge of the village, my dad, unlike most coffee growers in Agadji, had enough space to dry his entire harvest at home. Other farmers had no choice but to dry some pods on their farms, risking that some would be lost to thieves.

Coffee pods under normal weather conditions take seven to ten days to dry. The coffee drying season always coincided with the beginning of summer, allowing the heat, which was over 80 degrees on the sunny days, to dry the pods. During this process, the red, yellow, or green colors slowly turned darker and eventually black.

The test commonly used by farmers to see whether the pods were sufficiently dried was shaking a handful of the drying bean husks close to the ear. When the husks had dried enough, the farmers heard the noise of the beans rattling inside the husk.

The coffee was laid out to dry in three or four locations around our home. The thinner the layer of husks exposed to the sun, the faster they dried. As the coffee husks with the beans still inside dried, they were transferred to our silos or bagged. Once these were moved, their space was soon filled with new ones.

Once all the coffee of the harvest had been dried, it was taken to the nearest coffee mill in the village where it was husked.

The coffee mills, manufactured in England and Germany, have two main parts: the gas/oil engine and the milling mechanism. They cost between $2,000 to $3,000, which in my currency is between one and two million. The price of coffee mills, since their introduction to Togo, has always been out of the reach of individual farmers. Even today it is rare to find a farmer who owns a coffee mill in my region.

In the past, the few mills that existed were owned by a small number of businessmen. These businessmen provided an important service to the farmers who must, of course, in turn pay a fee. Payment was made in one of two ways. Either the farmer paid cash (highly unlikely), the exact amount depending on the quantity to be processed, or the mill operator kept a quarter of the beans to be husked. Business and profits were always very good for the mill owner, especially in villages like mine, where there were only two or three coffee mill owners and competition was almost nonexistent.

While the mill operator easily husked coffee for five to ten farmers in one day, it took all day and sometimes all night to husk my father's. The size of my father's harvest was well known in my village. When they heard that my father was having his coffee husked, the villagers stayed away from the mill. They knew it would be at least twelve hours before they would have a chance to have their coffee husked. Because my father didn't like holding other farmers up in getting their work done, he always made arrangements with the mill owner ahead of time, and the news always spread through the village.

In a typical harvest season, we started the trip to the mill around five thirty in the morning so that when the mill operator started around six, it would be there waiting for him. During the process, the whole family spent the whole day going back and forth between our home and the mill until all the coffee was husked and transported back home. All day we did only two things: take the coffee to the mill from home or carry the beans back home from the mill.

In my village, nothing is wasted, so the day after the husking was completed, my siblings and I helped our mother transport the coffee husks home from the mill. The husks were burned to ash. These ashes were then sold to women in the village who used it to make a traditional local soap called Akoto.

The coffee was husked before being sold so that the good beans could be separated from the bad ones. Screening consists of separating the black or bad beans from the gray or good ones. To help screen and sort my dad's coffee, the day after the husking, my mom again hired good women workers. Most families do their own screening, but my dad's harvest is too large. If we tried to complete the sorting by ourselves, it would take weeks before we'd be finished.

Because people knew my father would be hiring help, women well known by my parents as loyal and good workers had started applying to help my family screen our coffee before we had transported it home from the mill.

When it was time for the beans to be screened, the women my mother had hired would arrive early, usually around seven in the morning. These women came to our home sometimes with their teenage children to help them transport the beans.

Before my mother would distribute the beans, she made sure the women knew the wage that my father had set for the work. My father always set his wage a little higher than other coffee growers in the village in order to gain and maintain the loyalty of his helpers and to get better quality work from them.

Once the women knew what they would be paid for their work, my mother used a can to carefully measure the amount of beans distributed to each woman. The amount of coffee beans that mother allowed a worker to take home to be screened varied according to the woman's level of loyalty to our family. The more loyal, the bigger the amount she received and, consequently, the more money she made.

The women and their children carried the beans to their homes where they did the screening. When they were done, they brought the screened beans back to our home where my mother again measured them carefully and then paid the women for their much appreciated labor.

Once the coffee beans were screened, my father either transported them to the local government-appointed coffee buyer's shop or an agent came to our home. Again, because of the size of my father's harvest, most often buyers came to our house and transported the coffee to their shops at their own expense.

While my father received special attention from the buyers because of the size of his crop, there was no special consideration when it came to prices. At the beginning of each season, the government set the price "per kilogram" that could be paid for coffee. There were only two prices: a higher one for the good beans and a second lower one for bad beans known as déchés, which means bad beans. These prices were in effect until the end of a season. The buyers turned them beans over to the governmental agency, OPAT, which paid them bonuses depending on the volume of their purchases. The OPAT then exported the beans to the international market.

*****

As you can see, many people make a living from coffee. The ones who make the most are often the middle men and not the ones who put their life into raising the crop.

The sad reality of growing coffee in my country is that even big coffee farm owners, like my father, don't make a really good living regardless of how they work hard all year-round. My father, for example, in a good harvest year makes somewhere below $3,000. Though this is a good income by Togo standard, unfortunately, by the time he is done paying his expenses for fertilizer from OPAT, for workers, and such, he only has about $1,000 left.

Though $1,000 in Togo is considered to be a lot of money, I strongly believe that my father, for all the effort he and his family put into their farms all year-round, deserve more. Still, because of his revenue, my father has been able to send us children to private schools and to buy us clothes and shoes whenever we needed them. The average coffee grower in my village, who only makes about $200 in a good, productive season, could not afford to do as my father has.

*****

Most coffee growers who live mostly in Third World countries like Togo do not make enough to pull their heads above water, let alone keep a roof over their heads. In fact, the income level of hard-working coffee growers in Brazil and Central America is the same as that of the growers in my country—poverty.

An interesting question is: why is this so? How come these hard-working people make so little money growing coffee, especially when so many people in the world consume their product?

Well, there are several reasons.

First of all, the international coffee prices have always been kept very low to keep consumers happy. What I mean is that the price paid by the coffee companies to the governments of the countries that export coffee is kept low. To make that possible, the price paid to the actual farmer who nurtures the coffee as it grows is even lower. This manipulation of the price allows companies that sell coffee to the consumer and big international coffee trade corporations to make money that under fairer circumstances would go to hardworking coffee growers around the world, people like my own father.

If we would put ourselves in the shoes of those poor hard-working coffee growers, we might feel just a little of the frustration they feel of watching the price of coffee price drop each year—all for the benefit of the consumers like my friends here in the United States and owners of international coffee trade agencies such as the Organization of Coffee Exporting Countries (ODEC), who, for the most part, don't have a clue how hard it is to grow one coffee plant, let alone have a clue what a coffee plant looks like.

As a son of one of the best coffee growers in the entire world, I understand why a Colombian coffee grower would be tempted to grow marijuana or plants used to make cocaine and other illegal drugs instead of trying to grow more and more coffee. These farmers feel they must make a decision between continuing growing coffee and remaining poor or to switch to growing illegal plants and make much, much more money. The determination of the US government to arrest and punish poor farmers in Central and South America is a clear indication they don't understand the real dilemma that those farmers face every day.

It is ironic that some individuals in international trade organizations have become so wealthy they don't even know what to do with their money. They did not achieve their wealth from hard work but off the work of the farmers. Meanwhile, the hardworking coffee growers are becoming poorer and poorer with every single day that passes.

All I'm asking the international trade commission to do is to show some fairness to those poor farmers, especially those in Third World countries such as Togo. The need for a change is obvious. All we have to do is listen to the cries of coffee growers in poor developing countries. Listen to the suffering and the agony of that poor Colombian farmer who, because he grew illegal plants to survive and to support his family, sits behind bars, serving his jail term or waiting powerlessly for his death sentence.

Let's have a little justice in the trade system, a little balance in the profit sharing of the coffee trade. It can be done. We all know how dear a morning cup of coffee is to the average American. We could make a start with the consumer. If each coffee drinker throughout the world would accept a small increase in the price of a cup of coffee, a difference would be made. Then if the profiteering international coffee organizations would stop cheating those poor, hardworking coffee growers by cutting them out of the profit sharing or reduce the margin of their own profit by one-third to one-half, poor nations, like my own, whose economies rely heavily on income from agricultural exports would start making economic progress. Then developing countries, instead of asking for assistance or "a handout" from wealthy Western countries, could take care of themselves. Only if such an effort or commitment is made by the Western world will a Colombian farmer be less likely to abandon his coffee farms for the growing of illegal plants. And all this good could occur as a result of a small increase in the price of a cup of coffee. Amazing!

Another reason coffee grower are still the poorest of farmers in developing countries is that they haven't been able to have any real control over the trade of their coffee. In Western African countries such as Ghana, Ivory Coast, and Togo, the government has a tight hold on the production of coffee and other important export crops such as cocoa, cotton, corn, peanut etc. It is these governments whose agricultural agencies buy the crops from the farmers at prices below those paid on the international market. This significantly cuts the margin of profit that farmers would make if allowed to sell their products directly to international markets, perhaps through nongovernmental farmers' associations or agencies.

In Togo, for example, the profit margin for farmers has been significantly reduced over the last ten years, and to make matters worse, the price of fertilizer has tripled over the same period. Each year in my country, farmers, including my father, spend more than one-third of their profits on fertilizers. This once more explains why farmers are left with little to save by the time expenses and debts are paid.

The Togolese government not only controls the coffee prices but also the lives of coffee farmers. Farmers who grow cocoa, cotton, peanuts, and other crops for export are totally under the control of the government. The control is exercised through the national agency called the Togolese Office of Agricultural Products (OPAT). Though OPAT was established with the specific purpose of protecting farmers, due to the greediness of some very corrupt government officials, it now only exploits farmers.

While it's clear that local governments are not 100 percent responsible for the misery of coffee growers, or farmers in general, they still could treat them more fairly, and more importantly, they could also do a better job of pressuring the international trade organizations to raise the price of coffee and other crops to a more reasonable level.

*****

The final result is that in Togo, even though farmers put a great deal of effort into growing coffee, payment from the harvest barely allows them to pay off debts incurred the year before. If they're lucky, they might have a little leftover to help solve some of their family's financial problems and they might even be able to save a little.

If any coffee grower in my country can honestly claim that, despite all the difficulties, the coffee growing business has been beneficial to him, my father is clearly one. Even though my family's living standard still qualifies as poor, clearly, my father has been able to pull his family's head a little above the water. Due to his hard work and good management sense, my father has been able to send all four of his children to both public and private school—something no other farmer in Agadji has done.

In 1988, my dad's financial management also allowed him to finally save enough money to buy his first coffee mill, fulfilling a dream of many farmers in our Plateaux region; then in 1990, he purchased a second coffee mill, which is something unheard of. God willing, my dad looks forward to buying more mills in the years to come.

In the region where I grew up, buying a coffee mill is like buying a cab—very few people can afford either one. Most people who buy them do so with the idea of providing a service and making money. My dad's decision to buy the mills was not primarily to make money off his fellow farmers; it was to provide them a service and make their hard lives a little easier. Some farmers had to transport their coffee three or four miles from their farms to have it husked. My father's located his two mills within the farmers' communities, about ten miles from our village. In addition to his own coffee farm a mile from our Megbeadzre house, Father had coffee farms up the mountains about fifteen miles away, where he installed one mill on the compound of his main farm headquarters, right in the middle of his coffee farm. With his two mills about five miles apart, farmers who lived far from Agadji only had to travel a few miles now to have their coffee husked.

<u>In all fairness, I can say that my dear father always had at his heart, the best interest of his family, by always providing well for them and by always doing right by his farming community, creating job opportunities to the ones in need. A generous man; a wonderful man.</u>

*****

Even today, during harvest, not only does my father oversee his farms, but he also runs one mill, husking coffee for farmers. My brother Fidel, who helps our dad in his coffee business, manages the second mill five miles away.

At age sixty-five, my father is still as strong and as ambitious as ever. He has full control over the management of his farms, as well as of his family's daily affairs. Those who have had the chance to meet my father always wonder if he is ever tired, stops, or takes a break from working. The answer is a resounding no. My father and my entire family will agree with me—he does not know how to take a break. Maybe he does get tired like anybody else, but his willingness to be a strong role model for his children and to solve his family's financial problems is so great that he refuses to use fatigue as an excuse to slow down.

While the family worries about my dad's physical health problems that his overwork might cause, my dad worries about his coffee plantations. He is truly addicted to working, especially on his coffee farms.

Some minor health problems have slowed him down a little these past few years. In February 1991, he had a hernia operation. He was fortunate to be in an Italian-run hospital in Afagna, a city about twenty miles from Lome and sixty miles from Agadji. In 1995, he had surgery in the regional hospital in Lome, the capital of Togo, this time for an ulcer that nearly killed him. Even though my father has—thank God—fully recovered, we are all concerned that he rest more and be certain to recover all his strength.

There are people in my village that deserve my respect, and I do respect them a lot, but I have more respect for the man that I know as my father than for anybody else. I really don't know how to express the love, admiration, and respect I have for Mr. Koffi Edoh Otio Igneza Nicolas Adade. This respect is not only because he happened, by pure accident, to become my father. The truth is, everybody in my village, young and old, relatives and foreigners, who knows my father admires his thoroughness as a farmer, and, above all, his lovable, humble personality.

My father has met many people from other countries, among them US Peace Corps volunteers to Togo who were assigned to live in our village, people like Tom Buchanan, Russel Tomlin, Lynn Thomas, Trish Galligan, Maureen McCann, and Cindy Burns. These people lived or visited their fellow peace corps volunteer friends who lived near our Megbeadgze home. Through Tom Buchanan, he met Margaret and Verne Berry of Kalamazoo, Michigan, their older daughter, Joan, and her boyfriend, Charlie, who said they had to visit Togo to meet that "incredible man" and his family that a friend had told them about. When I was on a plane home from a visit to Tom Buchanan in Italy in 1987, I met an Italian couple, Guisseppe Giardini and wife, who were taking their honeymoon in Africa. I told them about my family and invited them to visit, which they did a week later. Dan Lawers, a friend from Kalamazoo and former assistant director of the Kellogg Foundation in Battle Creek, Michigan, spent three days with my family in Agadji during a business trip to four African countries in 1994. All of these people have remarked on how special and impressive my father is.

My father has a lot of dignity and very humble. His dignity and the respect of his fellow villagers do not necessarily come from his hard work on his farms; they come from his honorable social behavior; his respect for others, traditions, and his family; his positive thinking; his love for social justice; and his willingness to help whenever and wherever needed.

I just want to say one more time, and I will never say it enough, that we all love you, dear Father.

(End of Chapter 1)

Chapter 2

To My Dear Mother

My mother, like my father and 99 percent of villagers my parents' age, doesn't know exactly what year she was born in. When she was born, the idea of keeping birth records was totally unheard of in my small, spread-out farming community. There was no such person as a doctor or nurse around to deliver babies. They were delivered at home by or with the help of elderly women who, because of their wisdom and experience, fulfilled the role of midwife. Because nobody knew how to read or write, no written records were kept. The only thing that was done was to name the baby. Again, as in many tribes, the African names given to babies by the Akposso tribe into which my mother was born refer to the day of the week.

Also, during those days, there weren't such things as identification cards or drivers' licenses for the average Togolese.

Even though I personally find it regrettable that my parents don't know the month and year of their birth, I give credit to those African tribes like my own that gave each child a name based on the day of the week on which they were born, clearly reflecting a notion of time unlike that in the Western world. Though the younger generation and some Westerners might find that way of life a little backward, even funny, to people of my mother's generation, it was just the way things were done.

We all have the potential to see the ways of others as "odd." My generation finds it funny that when it comes to birthdays, Westerners, despite their long tradition of keeping records of birthdays, know only the date of their birth. Ask anyone in the Western world what day of the week they were born, and 99.9 percent of them won't know. Ask the same question of a three-year-old child in my tribe, the answer will come instantly. All this child has to do is remember his African name, and it will be clear what day he/she was born on.

I find it ironic that Americans love to celebrate the date of their birth, even though they have no clue which day of the week they were born. I think what Westerners really celebrate is not their birthdays but their birthdates.

My mother's African name is Ekoua, which indicates that she was born on a Wednesday. A female born on a Wednesday can also be called Akoua or Akouvi. My mother's Christian name is Elisabeth, and her nickname is Agbave, meaning in Akposso "a very light-skinned lady."

Unlike my dad, my mother was raised in a solid family with her parents present to raise her and teach her well. My mom's dad had two wives. Even though her own mother never had sons, my mom did have four half brothers. Also, unlike my dad's parents who were full-time farmers, my mom's father was a full-time carpenter and only a part-time farmer. Her father spent most of his time at home doing his carpentry work, while his wives did the everyday work on the farms.

As in many African countries, polygamy is allowed in Togo. Though many Westerners are disgusted by the practice, I have come to understand that this way of life is socially permitted primarily for economic reasons. Polygamy allows the man to have as many children as possible to help him on his farms.

Luckily, in most cases, wives and their children get along very well with one another, and therefore, I'm tempted to say that polygamy actually promotes a sense of solidarity and unity in the family. Unfortunately, polygamy is not always positive. The strongest argument I have against polygamy is that it is very difficult for a husband to treat all his wives and their children equally. Often the most attractive and youngest wife gets everything from the husband, while the less pretty and older ones are treated as faded flowers. Though the husband is required by social custom to look after his wives and children, the less popular ones are likely to get less from their husband than the favorite.

I do agree that while polygamy is widely accepted among my people and while most women manage to survive and even thrive under its rules, the less fortunate women are victimized by it. In the most unfortunate situations where divorce occurs, the woman most often loses custody of her children to her now former husband. Only very young kids are permitted to stay with their mother and then only until they are old enough to leave her, and then they move to their father's house.

The reasons for divorce are numerous. Most of the time, divorce happens when the man simply stops loving the woman and decides to marry a "more attractive or younger one." Divorce can also break up a household where the wives not only do not get along with one another but also fight like cats and dogs.

In the African society where children play many important roles, helping on the farms and with domestic work is very important. Above all, children represent the heirs of the traditions and the seeds of future generations, so the pressure on wives to bear their husbands' children is beyond imagination. A wife who fails to bear children is in most cases "condemned" to be divorced. Furthermore, wives must bear their husband at least one son, for in my Akposso tribe, sons are considered the true heirs of the family, the ones who will expand the family name and pass it on to future generations. A family without sons is considered a weakened family, a burning candle destined to be extinguished, a lost cause, so to speak.

The difficulties of polygamy can be seen in the life of Mrs. X, whom I remember as a very friendly young lady from Eketo village, one of the many small mountain villages about twenty miles from my village, Agadji. Mrs. X was known to be a good person and to have a sweet heart by most of my villagers. She was at first loved and well taken care of by my uncle, Mr. K, and his family.

Mr. K was a top employee in the governmental department that supervised the cotton growers in our region. Due to his influential job, he was not only well known but also able to seduce as many young women as he wanted: Mrs. X was one of his conquests. Though he never traditionally or officially married Mrs. X, they had a good life together, especially during and shortly after the birth of Mr. K's first son, P. Unfortunately, this good time only lasted until my uncle K fell in love with another woman in the neighboring village of Hiheatro, meaning in the Ewe dialect "the world has changed."

Though Mrs. X's friendliness never changed, it was obvious that she was not willing to share her man, my uncle, with another woman. I remember Mrs. X sharing her sadness with my mother, one of her closest in-laws. I am sure my mom gave her a lot of advice and comfort, but I'm not sure whether or not my mother was able to truly understand what Mrs. X was going through. My mother had never experienced that type of life with my father: she was my dad's only wife.

Before she knew it, Mrs. X was facing a big dilemma—leave my uncle and risk losing custody of her only child, who had ironically grown very close to his father or tough things out, trying to live with the situation. Like most mothers do in similar circumstances, she decided to stay for her son's sake, planning to stay at least until he was old enough to care for himself. Mrs. X was also hoping that her situation might eventually improve; instead, a tragic thing happened.

In polygamous families like the ones that exist in my tribe, men are socially obliged to look after their wives and children while wives are more directly responsible for the care of their own children. Failure to care for one's children can also be the cause for divorce.

Mrs. X's little boy, P, was seven, a very healthy and outgoing little boy who enjoyed life to the fullest. One Sunday, shortly after noon, the village was peaceful. The Adade family had just finished eating lunch, and almost everybody, even my father, was getting ready to kick back and take a nap. When an aunt came to announce to my mother that her brother's son, P, was not feeling well and had been taken to the medical center in Amlame. That evening when my mother visited little P, he seemed to be doing fine, but overnight his condition quickly deteriorated. The great care and love that the heath care workers and his mother gave him could not save his life.

Monday at dawn, little P passed away in his poor mother's arms. Mrs. X was more than devastated; little P represented everything to his mother. He was the only valuable thing in her life; he was the only reason she had decided to tough things out, hoping that things would get better with my uncle.

Four months passed and Mrs. X tried very hard to improve her relationship with my uncle. Unfortunately, my uncle's attention had long turned toward the new woman that he was dating. When it finally became clear to Mrs. X that she had failed to regain my uncle's attention, she put an end to her sorry love adventure with my uncle. One morning, Mrs. X packed her belongings and, after saying a heartbreaking goodbye to my mother as well as to others who were close to her, returned to her village.

While in some respects I disagree with polygamy, by the same token, I personally find it a more honest way of life than the supposedly monogamous Western arrangement that allows Westerners to marry, have children, and then divorce and remarry as many times as they choose. This lifestyle, I believe, breaks down the unity of the family. A child of a man who divorces the child's mother, whatever the reason, will rarely grow up close to any half siblings his father or mother may produce for him.

In the United States of America, divorces are frequent; people "legally" get married, divorced, and remarried within a very short period of time with or without having children. Is this not a form of polygamy? I sometimes wonder if Americans might not be more honest with themselves and even better off if they adopted polygamist beliefs and practices like those supported by many Africans, Muslims, and Mormons.

I hope you, dear reader, do not think I'm intending to be critical of the way Americans choose to live their lives. All I'm trying to do is suggest that some ways of living seem to fit well in one culture but not in another; that is life, that is reality. Like any civilization, Africa has its own reality as well.

One of the realities of life in Africa is that wives have to work hard to give their children what the husband is unable to provide them with, and the wives often must provide for themselves as well. Even though solidarity is the way of life in farming communities, as it is in my village, and even though the philosophy of solidarity is reinforced in polygamous families, the women are encouraged to find their own work to help support themselves and their children.

For instance, in addition to the family having the husband's farms, which benefit everyone in the family equally, each wife is encouraged to have her own side farms, her own silos, to provide an independent source of food. In my village, men concentrate on growing yams, cassava, coffee, and cocoa while women are growing corn, peanuts, beans, millet, fonio, and other cereal grains.

*****

My mother was more fortunate than my father in having parents and siblings around her when she was growing up. However, like my father, she never got a chance to go to school. Not being able to attend school was not due to a lack of family support, as was in my dad's situation. Simply put, my mother was female. During the '40s and '50s among the Akposso, the small Western-style schools were attended almost exclusively by males. Though this situation might have been different in other ethnic groups in Togo, at the time, that was the way it was for my mother.

Both parents opposed females attending school. Though European missionaries and the government encouraged women to get a school education, parents succeeded in maintaining the status quo for the longest time. The status quo involved believing that women existed only to be domestic creatures to marry, have babies, stay home, cook, and take care of housework. Sending females to school was considered a waste of money because when they got married, they would leave their father's home. The investment that a family had made in their daughter would be gone as she followed her husband. As a result, the parents, especially the father who in most cases is the one with the financial power, resisted the idea of sending daughters to school.

In addition to the fact that daughters would leave, parents feared their daughter might become pregnant by teachers or fellow students. A pregnancy would not only jeopardize the daughter's own future but would also represent a waste of the money that the family had invested in her, as she would become unmarriageable.

No, in my mother's days, the education of females in the family wasn't even discussed; the topic was essentially taboo. Today that way of looking at females' place in society has significantly improved; unfortunately, by the time it has changed, thousands of women had already been victimized by it.

My mother, like many other women who were unluckily born at that time, paid a costly price. She was flatly denied education. While her half brothers were being sent to the local school, my mother was forced to spend her time helping her mother on the farm, slowly but surely waiting for her only destiny—to get married and have children.

At seventeen, my mom was sent to Ghana, like my father, to become a seamstress. This type of education was more acceptable for females than formal education because it represented a short-term financial investment for the family on which they could be relatively certain of receiving a return. While it might take a very long time for her to graduate from a Western style school under normal conditions, one could complete an apprenticeship in about three years.

During her five years in Ghana, my mom had an easier time than my dad did. My mother didn't have to work side jobs to support herself. Also, my mother had the full support of her entire family. In addition to teaching my mother how to sew women's clothes, her boss lady in Ghana had a side business—baking. So my mom learned how to bake bread and how to sell it.

My mom recalls how every Saturday and Sunday she went to marketplaces to sell bread for her boss. Like my dad, my mom was well liked and respected by her boss because she worked hard, did her job well, and had good behavior.

My mother was twenty-two when she returned home to Agadji. When she arrived it was clear she was mature enough to be married. Her return coincided with my dad's visit from Tomegbe where he had just settled as a Ghanaian trained tailor. It didn't take long before my mom and dad caught each other's attention. They had a lot in common: they were from the same village and belonged to the same tribe: they had both just returned from Ghana and were beginning lives as professional tailors. They were about the same age with my father only eight years or so older than my mom. They were both young. and very attractive.

My father did not waste any time. As soon as some chemistry had started between them. he made the decision to marry her before he would return to Tomebge. My dad was in love. My father had never been so happy in his entire life. A young attractive woman my mother was, indeed. In addition to her beauty, what really tickled my dad's fancy was her very light skin color. My mother. like her father. was very light skinned. While the Akpossos in general. have a reputation in Togo of being light skinned. I have wondered whether my morn's father may have had white genes in his background. All I know is that my mom is one of the lightest skinned high yellow people in my entire village. My dad. no matter how tough he thought he was. couldn't resist my mother's beauty. and I can understand that.

Shortly after my clad decided that Akoua was the woman he loved and wanted to marry, he contacted his family members to follow all the traditions required to ask for her hand. He even delayed his return to Tomebge to finalize the wedding plans.

As has always been done in my tribe, the bride's family is contacted by the groom's special envoy to tell them that their son and their daughter are in love and willing to get married. After consulting with the bride to verify the truthfulness of the envoy's statement, a date is set for the groom's family to come and pay the dowry.

Now, in some tribes or ethnic groups in my country. the bride is not consulted at all. The marriage is handled among families like a business with marriages being strictly arranged. The men have the ultimate power to make decisions without the bride's approval, and the bride is literally forced to swallow the marriage decision made on her behalf by her family.

Even though arranged marriages do exist among my Akposso people, too, the bride is at least consulted. Her opinion does count.

My dad and my mom's love was true love. It was not arranged. In fact, before the envoy arrived, my mother had already paved his way. She had told her mother, Mrs. N'Koumenya, about her lover, my father; she had told her mother about her burning desire to marry this man. She told her mother this a few weeks before her then boyfriend's family had made any move. My mom decided to do this to give her mother time to observe her lover for herself and make her own evaluation.

My grandmother N'Koumenya couldn't resist the charm or the good behavior of her daughter's lover. She observed and re-observed my father but could not come up with any reasonable motive to oppose the relationship. Maybe Mrs. N'Koumenya couldn't find anything bad being said about my dad in the village because very little was known about him. After all, he had just returned after spending many years in Ghana and was now living in Tomegbe.

Or maybe not finding negative information about him was due to Mrs. N'Koumenya's easygoing nature. I myself had the privilege and honor of knowing my grandma firsthand and admiring her. I remember the great love that Grandma surrounded me and my siblings with when we were growing up.

I also remember how mad my older brother Fidel and I used to make our grandma by sneaking into the orange tree that was six meters from her mud house bedroom. Fidel and myself really didn't mean to give her a hard time. It was just that that particular orange tree produced the sweetest oranges in the whole country of Togo. Grandma always got furious at us for climbing that orange tree because it belonged to Mr. Apedo, her second husband, the one she married after the death of my mom's dad. Though Mr. Apedo himself never protested our interest in his orange tree, our grandma tried to keep us away from it to show respect for her husband. In addition, she didn't want to have to tell our parents if we injured ourselves while climbing.

Regardless of how furious she was, Grandma never raised her voice; instead, she used her unique talent of persuasion to discourage us from being bad. This tactic worked for a while, especially when we were little, and then she distracted us with pennies, sweets, and other things that attract little kids' attention. But as we grew up, her little tricks no longer worked, so she resorted to scaring us. Grandma asked a neighbor to hang a funny-looking object in the tree. She told us the object was voodoo and would cause us to lose our fingers if we dared touch any more oranges without her approval. That trick kept us away from that orange tree until we were old enough to understand that those "voodoo" objects were nothing but jokes.

It was always very pleasant being around Grandma N'Koumenya. She passed away in 1986, and we still miss her dearly.

*****

For whatever reason, my dad easily passed his test with my grandmother, Mrs. N'Koumenya. Convinced that my dad was an honest, honorable young man with a good head on his shoulders, she determined he would make a good husband for her daughter, and Mrs. N'Koumenya Essousso went out of her way to let her husband, Mr. Doumessi Etse, know what was going on. Mr. Doumessi Etse, eager to see some nice man marry his daughter, trusted his wife's words and did not oppose the marriage.

While my dad ran into no major opposition from most of his soon-to-be-family, there was one minor opposition.

Early one evening, around five thirty, my grandma, Mrs. N'Koumenya, went to visit her younger sister Ekpetsi, who, like most wives at that time of day, was starting to cook dinner when Mrs. N'Koumenya arrived.

"Ekpetsi, are you home?" yelled my grandma.

"Yes, I'm here in the kitchen," she replied.

"I have something very important to talk to you about," my grandma insisted.

Mrs. Ekpetsi came quickly out of her little kitchen, which was full of thick white smoke from the fire she had just lit.

"Come on in this other room. This smoke is too nasty," Mrs. Ekpetsi said. "Have a seat and tell me in a hurry what is going on. You seem very concerned, dear sister."

"Well," my grandma started, "I already know what your reaction will be, but I had decided to get your opinion on this family matter."

"Um, you know, my daughter Akoua is really in love with that Koffi Nicolas." She paused as if to check her sister's pulse.

"I know," Ekpetsi replied. "So what is new about it? I just hope you are not here to announce to me that they are planning on getting married." She hinted. "Just a second," she interrupted the flow of the conversation. "Adjoua, Adjoua," she called to one of her daughters, "go keep an eye on the stove for me, would you? I will be right out to start dinner."

"Um," my grandma continued, "see, what did I say? I knew it. I knew you would react this way, so I'm afraid to tell you that, indeed, Akoua and Koffi are planning on getting married. In fact, it's only a matter of days, and Koffi and his family are coming to ask for Akoua's hand."

"What?" Ekpetsi erupted. "I cannot believe that you are allowing this Koffi man to marry my niece. I cannot believe this! Tell me, what can this poor man do for my beautiful niece? Don't you see that she deserves a better man than this poor Koffi?"

"I really don't know what you are talking about," my grandma replied. "Akoua made her decision to marry Koffi herself. What do you want me to do? Don't you see that Akoua is old enough to decide what is good for her?"

"I guess I wish them good luck. At least, you make sure that Koffi brings us a good dowry. I'm sorry but I have to start cooking dinner now before my family starves to death."

"Have a good evening," my grandma said to her sister as she stomped off.

Due to my mom's attractiveness and pleasant nature, her aunt would have preferred that she marry an influential person with a lot of money. That my mother was marrying my father for love instead of material considerations really did not make sense to her auntie.

Considering the times, my mother's aunt did have good reasons. Since women were denied education and were raised only to become someone's wife, it was not bad thing for older women to wish their daughters and nieces to marry someone rich who could and would take good care of his wife and children. A woman who married a poor man might only not be well taken care of, but such a man also would not be able to pay his in-laws back some of their investment in their daughter. A woman who married a poor man was also more likely to keep coming back to her parents and family, seeking help of all kinds.

So as you can see, my mom's aunt wasn't being rude; her comment was understandable. Sadly, the woman couldn't focus on how much love my mom and my dad had for each other. Nor could she understand the resolve of this soon-to-be couple to fight any opposition and get married no matter what. That true love has no boundaries was not important in her world.

My grandmother, however, understood, and though she was fully aware that my dad and his family didn't have enough money to pay a good dowry for her daughter, she was willing to let her daughter marry my dad. She deeply believed that people make their own circumstances and that a poor person who works hard can become rich. In the same vein, she believed that a rich person who ceased to work hard could fall to the very bottom of the ladder and become poor. In addition, my grandmother understood that being born into a wealthy or poor family was not under the control of any child. Despite his lack of money, my grandmother saw in my father a potentially hard worker, and that convinced her that even if my dad didn't become very wealthy one day, he would work to put food on the table for her daughter and her grandchildren. As it turned out, Mrs. N'Koumenya had a correct vision of my dad.

A couple of weeks passed after Mrs. Ekpetsi and my grandma's conversation during which Ekpetsi unsuccessfully tried to make my mother change her mind.

Despite Ekpetsi's efforts, the day for my father to formally ask for my mother's hand arrived. In the Akposso tribe, these very special visits only take place at dawn, so at sunrise on that fateful morning, my dad and six members of his family—three men and three women—knocked at the door of my mother's father, Mr. Doumessi Etse. My dad and his family brought with them one bottle of Sodabi, the local brandy made from palm wine, and a bottle of Schnapps, one of the fanciest and most expensive brandies imported from Europe.

147

In addition to being presented at wedding proposals, Schnapps, Gordon Gin, European wines, or the local Zota and Sodabi are only used at specific, special occasions. During wedding negotiations, they are used as a way of paying the dowry. They are also used at funerals and during visits by important guests. When villagers meet to settle disputes, the person found guilty pays the other side with the drink.

*****

A few minutes after my dad and his escorts arrived at the bride's home, the bride's family members, especially the elderly people previously contacted about this matter, started arriving too.

On these occasions, the highest level of respect is shown to the elderly members of the tribe. They are treated as wise ones, sometimes even like kings and queens. To solidify the role, one temporary elderly spokesperson is chosen in each family. These spokespersons do the most talking, serving as intermediaries between the two families.

As soon as they were all seated, the head of my father's delegation greeted the assembly, telling the bride's family the reason for their visit. It was then that my mother and grandmother were brought into the meeting. My mother, as if she were not aware of her destiny, was told by her father's spokesperson the purpose of the meeting.

As soon as my mother and her mother were seated, their family spokesperson got up and addressed her, "Ekoua, do you know the young man sitting over here named Koffi?" pointing his right hand at my dad.

"Yes, Uncle. I know him," replied my mother in an unusually shy tone.

"Do you know him very well?" insisted the spokesperson. "Yes, Uncle, I know him very well," answered my mom. As if the forthright spokesperson didn't quite understand my mother's answers, was waiting for a different answer, or perhaps simply wanting to make sure he was doing his assigned job well, he continued his chain of questions more aggressively. "How well do you know Koffi?"

My mother wasn't quite comfortable with this question, but instead of showing anger toward her spokesperson uncle, she told everybody (present) what she had confided to her mother two weeks earlier. "Um...um, he is my lover."

"Good," the spokesperson said with satisfaction; things were going well. "Ekoua," he continued, "your lover, Koffi, and his family are here this morning for only one reason, as you can imagine, to ask for your hand. Your own father and your mother would like to know if you accept their request and want to marry Koffi."

"Yes, Uncle," my mother responded without hesitation.

"I'm sorry. I didn't hear you clearly, Ekoua," said the spokesperson jokingly, pretending he had forgotten to turn his hearing aid on.

"Uncle," said my mom politely, "please tell my parents that this is the man that I love. This is the man that I want to marry. My answer is yes."

Reassured that everything was okay with my mother, the spokesperson turned quietly and bent over almost to the ground as a sign of respect and reported back to my mom's father that his daughter agreed to marry Koffi. He then turned and reported to my mom's mother in the same fashion.

Next, addressing my father's family, the spokesperson said, "As we have all witnessed, our daughter, Ekoua, has accepted your proposal and is willing to become your son Koffi's wife. We, Ekoua's family, have nothing else to say or do but to respect our daughter's will."

At this moment, the head of the delegation of my dad's family briefly consulted with their spokesperson, who, in a very swift and precise manner, stood up and addressed the bride's family:

"We don't have anything to say other than to thank you all, especially your daughter, Ekoua, for accepting our son, Koffi, as her husband. As we all know, it's always a great pleasure to see our sons and daughters marrying each other. We are all the same people in this village."

With a quick, smooth action, the groom's spokesperson picked up a bag from next to his seat and handed it to the bride's spokesperson, addressing him, "This bag contains a bottle of Schnapps and

Sodabi. We offer it to you to officially mark the beginning of our special relationship through the union of our son, Koffi, and your daughter, Ekoua. Having said that, we would like to know what you require from us as dowry for your daughter."

The bride's spokesperson stood once more and requested a moment to consult with the other members of the delegation to come to a common decision. The bride's family stood and went into another room to set the dowry.

The break only lasted ten minutes. After returning from the private meeting, the bride's spokesperson gave a list of things they wanted from the groom's family. Among the items were a dozen pair of beautiful African cloth for the bride, two kente cloths for the bride's father, jewelry for the bride and her mother, two goats (a male and a female), one snow-white sheep, a specified sum of money, a big jug of local palm wine, and six more bottles of Sodabi.

Without discussion, my dad's family agreed to the dowry, and a date was immediately set to bring it to the bride's family.

To some extent, my mom became officially married at that meeting. Even so, it wasn't until the dowry was actually given in full to her family that she was allowed to move in with her husband; it was a very simple form of traditional wedding.

*****

The more traditional the wedding, the more time, money, and people are required. Such a wedding involves the entire village. For seven long days, the bride is treated like a queen by the entire village, especially the groom's family and her close relatives. During those days, all the bride is allowed to do is eat meals cooked by family members and look pretty.

She is dressed daily in very nice traditional outfits by the elderly women from either family. The outfits are made of either tradition-ally woven kente-like cloth or of two European fabrics called pagne, usually imported from Holland. Whatever the cloth, the bride always wears a nice white shirt along with the cloth. Also, the bride wears six or seven different colorful bead necklaces, handmade by the elderly women in the village; matching bracelets are worn on both of her wrists.

Relatives from both families take turns singing beautiful traditional songs for the bride; these songs last for at least twelve hours every single day and for a week. This special treatment is designed to make the bride feel like a true African queen or perhaps to encourage her to enjoy her last moments of celibacy before becoming a wife and entering the next stage of her life—motherhood.

Unlike the atmosphere during a funeral, during those seven long days, the whole village breathes, lives, and enjoys an atmosphere of joy and intense celebrations combined with deeply significant traditional rituals.

The bride's final departure from her parents' home to her husband's is marked by a dozen gun salute given by the hunters of the village. The salute is shot off either from the Odjani, the traditional place where most public ceremonies are held, or from the bride's home or simultaneously from both locations. The hunters may be dressed casually or wearing special hunters' outfits of a reddish color. The color makes the hunters' clothes look like they were dyed in the dried blood of the thousands of wild animals they have hunted over the years.

It is said of the hunters in my tribe that they rarely, if ever, wash their hunting clothes as a way of showing how good they are—the more bloody-looking their outfits are, the better hunters they are. These hunters wore similar outfits during intertribal wars before the European colonization. In those days, tribes fought one another for such reasons as control of territories, water supplies, fertile lands for agriculture, and areas in which wild animal herded.

*****

Unfortunately, my dad and his family didn't have the financial resources for such a celebration. My father may also have been anxious to return to Tomegbe and didn't want to stay long in the village. Remember, he had just been visiting from Tomegbe when he met and fell in love with my mother, Ekoua. Whatever the reason, it didn't really matter to my mother. What mattered to her was to be married honorably, and that she was. Clearly, my mother was happy with the small traditional ceremony she had. Yes, indeed, my dear mother, Ekoua, was a happy bride, and while she was not treated like a queen by the entire community for seven long days, we do treat her like a queen at home today.

While my mother always knew that my dad would be returning to Tomegbe soon, it was not until two weeks after their wedding, when the dowry had been presented in full, that he let his in-laws know of his decision to return to Tomegbe with his first and only wife, their daughter, Ekoua.

My mother, having already decided what to do with her life by marrying my father, had no objection to the idea of moving to Tomegbe. However, my mom's departure broke her mother's heart, not only because they were close but also because my mother had just returned from Ghana, and she and her mother hadn't really had time to enjoy each other's company enough. To mark her daughter's departure with a special fingerprint, my grandmother N'Koumenya accompanied my parents to Tomegbe to see with her own eyes the new home of her dear daughter. My grandmother stayed in Tomegbe for several days and then returned to Agadji, convinced that her daughter was safe in my dad's hands and those of his relatives in Tomegbe.

From day one of her marriage, my mother has always been loving, caring, and faithful to her husband, and my dad has been the same toward her. As a good wife, she has always enjoyed being at my dad's side in both good and bad times. No matter how bumpy my dad's road has been, my dear mother has always shared it with him. She has given my father all the strength, comfort, and advice he has needed and more; with this support, he has been able to overcome his, or rather their obstacles.

This doesn't mean that my mom has necessarily gone along with everything that my dad has said, done, or wanted to do. On many occasions, she has furiously opposed my dad when she felt he was about to make a bad decision. Because my mom has a great deal of influence and say in my father's dealings, he listens to her before making a final decision. Still, in a male-dominated society such as mine, most of the time, my mom abides by my dad's decisions.

*****

In Tomegbe, my mom was a full time housewife and mother, and her duties were to cook and take care of her husband and her children, the way all good housewives do in my West African country of Togo. She would sew once in a while for her first daughter, Pauline, but she never had the chance to make full use of her knowledge as a tailor, the way my dad did.

My dad was a full-time tailor, providing for the financial care of the family, while my mom was in charge of domestic work. It wasn't until my parents moved back to Agadji, and especially after my younger sister Jeanne, the last in the family, was old enough to go to school that my mother started working on the coffee farms with my dad.

During the long time she spent as a housewife, my mom did numerous odd jobs to help supplement the family income. Meals are not provided at schools in my country, so she cooked and sold food to school children during their lunch break. When my dad chopped down some palm trees, she made palm wine. In addition to the wine, my mom made some of the best red palm oil in my village, a skills she inherited from her own mother. She sold both at the local market.

While I was growing up, I watched my mother hold my family tightly together with her hard work and dedication. Because of this, I call her my hero. In Africa in general and in my tribe in particular, being a good wife is one issue; being a good mother is quite a different one. My mother has been both a good wife to my father and a wonderful mother to her children.

In my country, domestic abilities are considered the sine qua non or main qualities that women must have to be good wives. These abilities are the main criteria of beauty of an African woman and are the first qualities an African man looks for in a woman before even considering marriage. Be assured that an African woman who dares to hate domestic work will either have a hard time finding a good man to marry or simply be unmarriageable. No matter how pretty such a woman is, she will always have problems with her own family as well as with her in-laws if she does somehow manage to get married.

In addition, in my tribe, a husband who spends too much time in the kitchen doing his own laundry, doing his own dishes, or daring to do some grocery shopping is made fun of by the whole village, especially by the women. For instance, a man who does his own grocery shopping is called a stingy person—a man who is so stingy that he wants to know how much change is left after the shopping, a man who is too stingy to let his female relatives, wife, or girlfriend keep that change. While men don't go food shopping in my country, they do shop for other items.

Also, no man, especially not a man who was married, would ever do laundry in my tribe. Men always find a sister, cousin, niece, or a girlfriend or fiancée to do their laundry. Young boys may have to do their laundry once in a while, but once they pass puberty, they stop.

Because of this fear of mockery, men are taught at a very young age to stay away from female duties and only attend to their own socially acceptable duties such as working hard every day at whatever their jobs may be to support their families. In my tribe, a man who enjoys doing female duties and domestic tasks too much risks scaring women away and ending up a bachelor for the simple fact that no African woman wants to marry an effeminate or stingy man.

*****

As a good woman who respected her traditions regarding the duties of wives, domestic work was always on the top of my mother's daily schedule. She always made sure her husband and children had clean clothes to wear by doing laundry when it was needed. She kept busy in the kitchen, cooking and serving meals on time for my dad and the family. Making sure the kitchen was clean, especially the dishes, was a major job—one she didn't have to do by herself. Her children, especially her female children, would help, learning to be good wives themselves.

Once or twice a week, my mom went grocery shopping at the local outdoor marketplace or traveled to a surrounding village where the market was being held. She made sure she supplied her kitchen with food enough to last for four days to a week until the next market day came around. She always used the money my dad gave her wisely.

These are a few tasks my mom had to take care of on a daily basis in order to be considered a good wife, and she did them all without complaint.

*****

In addition to her household tasks, my mom took excellent care of us four children. Like any other good mother, my mom always made sure we wore clean clothes, ate well, and were on time. She never hesitated to take us to the health clinic in the neighboring village of Amlame whenever one of us wasn't feeling well. She always woke us up on time, made certain we washed, and got us ready to go to school, church, or wherever on time.

While she enjoyed spoiling us to show her love, whenever we misbehaved, my mom did not hesitate to punish us, trying to make it clear to us that life is not a bed made of roses and not to be taken lightly. As a result, like a good mother, she always knew how to play the role of both a good defense lawyer and a prosecution attorney when we got into trouble with our dad, who at times was too quick to show his muscles.

One night, when Fidel and I were in our early teens, Fidel almost got his butt kicked by our father. It was April, a week or so before Easter. For more than three days, the main topic of conversation among the villagers was about this band from Ghana on tour in our Akposso region that was going to do a play about the crucifixion of Jesus Christ. The village was full of talk about how talented the actors of this play were. The whole village was eagerly waiting to see the performance.

Early afternoon on a Friday, the "concert band" finally made it to our village as scheduled. That evening, my parents returned home from their farms a little earlier than usual in order to eat dinner and get ready to go see the play. My father, to the astonishment of us all, decided to be sociable and go with us. The play took place downtown, about a mile from our Megbadzre home. We left early because our father wanted to make sure that he got his money's worth for the tickets he had purchased.

As expected, we got some of the best seats. As predicted, the play was truly mind-blowing. While Jesus Christ was betrayed by one of his disciples, captured, beaten, tortured, and put to death by his own people, the actors made everyone in the audience feel every emotion, as if it were really happening. The play was so good and sad one didn't have to be a Christian to see how painful that ordeal was for Jesus. The majority of the audience, including my mother, were reduced to tears. Luckily, the end of the play, when Jesus Christ rose from the dead, brought great joy back into the hearts and souls of the villagers. This once-in-a lifetime experience lasted about three hours. As the play ended well after dark, around 10:00 p.m., families headed home, looking forward to a quiet night following the nice play.

Unfortunately, the quiet mood was to be interrupted for our Adade family; Fidel, following the play, disappeared. Instead of following our parents as Pauline, Jeanne, and I did, Fidel stayed behind in the village, chasing girls. We children were required to get our parents' approval before we did anything out of the ordinary. That night, Fidel stepped out of line, taking advantage of the positive atmosphere of the village following the play to satisfy his sexual drive.

While our parents might have given Fidel permission to stay had he asked, he didn't. Thanks to the play, maybe Fidel had run into some nice young girl that he would otherwise have had a hard time seeing at that time of the day. In small villages like Agadji, where everybody knows everybody and the villagers mostly trust one another, parents still manage to protect their children, especially their daughters, from engaging in sex in their early teen years and thus avoid teen pregnancies. I believe it was that strict parental supervision of children that induced Fidel that night to take advantage of a rare opportunity.

When we realized Fidel was gone, my father and I stayed behind for twenty minutes, hoping Fidel would show up so we could go home together, but we all returned home that night without Fidel. At first, we were all concerned that something bad had happened to him, but my parents decided not to panic. They probably suspected why Fidel had failed to return home with us, and if so, they were convinced it would be foolish to look for him, knowing that he would be taking all precautions to avoid being seen by anyone, especially his parents. Therefore, my parents decided to stay put until Fidel returned home. When my father and I returned home, my mom had already arrived with my two sisters, Pauline and Jeanne. She greeted us with a question.

"Where is your son Fidel?"

My father was too upset to talk and didn't answer. My mother, not satisfied, turned to me and asked again, "Peter," as she likes to call me, "where is your older brother?"

"I don't know, Mammi."

My father, who had disappeared into his house, came out carrying his Akpassa, meaning "lazy chair" in Akposso, and Ewe, a La-Z-Boy recliner in the hips. My father sat clown in his Akpassa chair, still not talking, determined to wait for the return of his "bad boy" son. My mom made two more unsuccessful attempts to get my father to talk. Then perhaps to distance herself from Fidel and appease my father, my mother tried a different tactic, declaring dramatically, "Fidel! Fidel is going to kill me! I wish he listened to my advice."

About an hour later, Fidel showed up, clearly satisfied with whatever good time he had had with his female friend. When he saw our father sitting in his Akpassa, his look of satisfaction turned to concern; he was scared that our father was waiting outside that late.

Clearly furious, my father declared, "Come here, Fidel."

Fidel, too scared to resist my father's order, approached. My father sprang up and was about to grab his son when, to cool my dad off a little, my mother came out of their living quarter and declared, "Fidel, what have you done?" Before Fidel had a chance to answer her question, she bombarded him with another question. "Tell me what time it is."

My father followed immediately with a third question: "Where have you been?"

By this time, Fidel knew he was in deep trouble, or as we say, "about to swim in hot water." Fidel didn't give any answer. Instead, he began looking around with a defeated look on his face, searching for compassion and forgiveness. What he got was a reaction from my mom, "Don't you look at me as if I encouraged you to do what you just did. Answer your father's question," perhaps suggesting her questions were less important than her husband's.

With a long hesitation due to not knowing what to say, Fidel decided to give some kind of answer before my father became even more upset and managed to stutter. "I...I...I..."

"I, I what?" interrupted my father.

"I was with, with...with X...I mean Y." (X and Y were male friends of his.) Both my parents were convinced that their son Fidel was hiding the truth. While my father was growing angrier and closer to disciplining Fidel on the spot, my mother was trying to think of a way to defend Fidel. She turned toward my father and said, "Honey, that is enough. It's getting too late, and you'll have to get up early in the morning to go to the farm. As you can see for yourself, your son feels sorry for what he has done. Enough of this. Please let him go to bed."

"What?" my dad erupted furiously, turning on my mother. "Let him go to bed after keeping me awake all this time? Did I just hear you ask me to let Fidel go to bed? Huh? Huh? What kind of signal would we be sending to his younger brother Pierre? That it's okay to behave the way his older brother just did? Huh? Huh? Answer me!"

My mother, unwilling to back down as she sometimes had, answered, "No, I did not say that, did I? All I'm saying is that it is getting too late, and I think your son needs to go to bed." At that point my mother did not wait for my father's comment before she ordered Fidel, "Tell your father you're sorry and go to bed. Look at you all scared and shaky. Never again doing anything unusual without first checking with your parents. Have a good night."

Fidel, empowered by his mom's defense, turned to his dad and quietly said, "I'm sorry, Papa." My father did not say a word. Fidel turned to his mom and said, "Thank you, Mammi…"

By then, it was clear to my father that he had lost the fight. His attempt to discipline Fidel on the spot had failed, but he went to bed satisfied with the way his wife had handled the situation because Fidel, following his mom's order, had come to him and said he was sorry.

*****

My mom's social life was more visible in my village than my dad's, or perhaps it would be better to say, more audible. My mom is always singing. Because of her interest, shortly after my parents moved back to Agadji from Tomegbe, my mother joined the village's, then only Catholic choir. Today there are two Catholic choirs, and my mom's choir still performs and is now called the senior choir.

Because of her clear voice, she sang first soprano. Her voice is also very strong and can honestly be heard miles away. Because of the uniqueness of her voice, whenever the choir performs whether at practice session or during Sundays or holiday services, myself and everyone in the village could always pick out my mother's voice.

I remember coming home one night with a date, one of my first girlfriends. Because this girl lived on the east side of town and me on the west side, to get home to Megbeadzre, we liked to walk in the dark main road, which ran next to the St. Augustine Church, where the choir was practicing that night. As we neared the church, my female friend became evasive in our romantic conversation. I realized that she was enjoying listening to the choir, which was singing one of her all-time favorites. The song was based on the twenty-third Psalm, "The Lord is my shepherd…" Because we both loved that religious song, we paused to soak it in before we continued our romantic walk. My friend suddenly got a funny expression on her face. When I asked her what the matter was, she paused and then asked me, "Your mom is not practicing tonight, is she?"

"Nope!" I responded. "She is home sick with a cold."

"No wonder," she continued. "The choir sounds different. Your mom has such a lovely voice. I can tell when she is singing with the choir."

Even though I hundred percent agreed with my friend about my mother's voice, I joked, "Did you just say my mother has a lovely voice? Wait until you hear her yell at me, then you can tell me what her voice is really like." We both laughed and continued our walk.

My mother's voice is still so clear that whenever she gets upset and starts yelling, she will make you regret ever upsetting her. My mom can still make me drop a glass of water when she yells at me when she catches me off guard.

Not only is my mom a good singer, she is also the most feared, trusted, and respected member of the choir. For more than a decade, she was the choir's treasurer or money keeper, which the choir needed because there was no bank in my village. On special holidays such as Christmas or Easter, after church service, the choir would go through the entire village from house to house singing their beautiful songs written in our native languages for Our Almighty God Jehovah and his son Jesus Christ. The choir also performed at weddings and funerals for which they received donations. The choir used the money to buy or repair drums or to buy new uniforms. Once in a while, they would organize a private party for members of the group.

The amount of money raised was enormous at times, and it was kept in a safe place by the chosen treasurer. The choir's money was kept in a very safe place, yet no matter when the choir needed some of it, they always had access to it through my mother. My dad was the only person beside my mother to know where the choir money was secreted away in our house.

On many occasions, my older brother and my older sister would help our mom in her duties as treasurer. However, perhaps because my mother understood very well that all children love toys and money, the way bees love their honey, she took no potentially embarrassing risks by trusting her children with that knowledge. My mother always managed to keep the money out of our reach, much as many people today keep chemical products away from children. My mom understood very well that even though her children were well taught and well behaved and would never touch anything that wasn't theirs, like other children, they might be tempted to steal or accidentally tell someone else where the money was hidden.

The only times I personally learned anything about the choir money was when the president of the choir or a designated member came to my mother to make a withdrawal and no one else was home. My mother would desperately need somebody to help her record the transaction. Only then would she ask me to write down the date, the amount being withdrawn, the name of the person withdrawing the money, and the new balance. My mom would then take that paper and disappear into her secret hiding place. In all those years, my mother never charged the choir for her services. The only benefit my mother received from this work was a reputation in the village as a good cashier, and maybe she also loved the sense of power that she had not only over the money itself but also over her fellow members. She may have felt special satisfaction about the power she had over the men in the choir, a small advantage in the heart of a society where only men have power in almost every aspect of life.

During the early '80s, an Akpe group from Amou Oblo, a neighboring village, was invited to perform in my village on Christmas. The performance of this group was so attractive and joyful that some villagers decided to start a dance group in our village; my mother was among them. My villagers were so inspired that within weeks, it became the most popular form of recreation for all of Agadji, and even expanded to include people from the surrounding villages, led by a young and a charismatic man named YAKPO.

The Akpe group, like a choir, meets almost every evening for rehearsal. One of their favorite times for rehearsal is the full moon. The moonlight is most useful, and the moon's heavenly beauty can really be appreciated in villages like mine where until recently there was no electricity.

One of the most exciting moments in the history of the Akpe occurred two years after it started up. The members did some intensive fundraising and purchased better, more suitable drums. The drums the group first used were borrowed from the village choir; they also, technically speaking, were not fit for the dance group. However, in the beginning, when the group had no money in its coffers, it had no choice but to borrow the choir drums. As the French proverb says, "A defaut de viande, on mange du poisson," meaning "If you don't have meat, it's okay to eat fish."

I remember the joy that filled the entire village for months after the arrival of those six different-sized drums, which had been ordered from a small village in eastern Togo near the city of Tsevie, meaning "let the crops produce a while before we move to a different location." The old drums had been carved from wood. These new ones were skillfully forged from light metal and then covered with dried animal skins; they produced much better sounds. When the new drums were brought to the village by a carefully picked delegation of members from the Akpe group, the percussion procession was accompanied by a very special metal horn used during the Akpe dance. The horn was used to signal a change of speed, direction, or style for the dancers.

That Sunday, the Akpesse dance started around two thirty in the afternoon and lasted until close to 8:00 p.m. That was indeed a joyful Sunday in my Adade family as in many others. My whole family was involved. That day, Fidel, my brother, was playing a drum. My sisters Pauline and Jeanne, my mom, and myself were busy dancing. My dad, as usual, was busy watching everybody have a good time. My father did eat a very late dinner that clay, but he didn't seem to mind.

Not long after the new drums arrived through other fundraising, the Akpe group was able to by two to three beautiful uniforms for each of its members. The villagers supported the group because their performances brought us such pleasure.

My mother, one of the founders of our Akpe group, became first the group's cashier and then president for five consecutive years in the early '80s.

Being involved with the Akpe group never prevented any men from maintaining her full membership in the choir. Soon after our family finished dinner, my mom went off to choir rehearsal, which usually finished around 8:30 p.m. Then she joined the Akpe rehearsal already in process and stayed there until 10:00 or 11:00 p.m. when she returned home. My father has never seemed to mind her time away from home as long as my mom remained a good wife and enjoyed herself.

Because of the small but honorable roles performed by my mom, we Adade children grew up with positive pressure to maintain the good reputation of our parents and family by behaving ourselves whenever and wherever we go.

As soon as my youngest sister, Jeanne, entered school, my mother started changing her daily domestic routine. After sending us to school, she joined my dad in his fields and worked with him until about 5:00 p.m. when it was about time for school to let out. Then she returned home to make sure we children arrived home safe and to get dinner ready by 6:30 p.m. when my dad returned.

By the time we had moved to our new home in Megbeadzre, my younger sister Jeanne was old enough to walk to school all by herself, and we children were taking such good care of each other that our mother felt certain we would be all right on our own. My mother's sense of reassurance also came from the fact that our school was only about ten meters from our house.

In 1974, when my dad finally decided to become a full-time coffee grower, my mother became a full-time farmer at her husband's side. Not only has she always helped my dad in his coffee farms, but she has also made sure our family has had enough grain in our silos to see us through the year and to make our bread. My mother has always teased my dad. "Koffi, you know, you only think about your coffee farms. Your children will starve to death if we don't manage to put some grain (rice, beans, fonio, etc....) in our silos." In fact, making sure we didn't starve has been my mom's first priority ever since my dad became a full-time coffee grower.

*****

Even though my dad is by far the hardest worker in the family when it comes to farming, my mother deserves a great deal of credit for her contribution to our family as a farmer. Even my dad knows this and always praises my mother for her everyday and every-year efforts.

Looking back on all the contributions my mother has made to her family as a wife and a mother, I really cannot imagine what my family would be like without the privilege of having her around. I don't know what I would have become without having her for a mother.

On behalf of my brother, Fidel; my sisters, Pauline and Jeanne; my father, Koffi Nicolas; as well as my nephews, Maxim, Koboe, Romeo, Serge, Kwame; my sons, Nico, Ethan, Nathan; their loving mother, Kimberly Hester; my nieces, Cherita, Ina, Chimene, Ida, Victoire; my brother-in-law, Gerson Yaovi Kouma; Romeo's mother, Jackie Douamegno, and my very Dear Friend Krystal Chanel Johnson. I just want to say these few words: we love you, Mother, and thank you so very much for everything you've done for us.

Chapter 3

To my siblings, my dear family, the villagers of Agadji say it all when they declare, "Nobody messes with Ekoua and Koffi Nicolas children. They are very polite and very well behaved."

Without any touch of arrogance, I have to agree hundred percent with these statements. Mrs. Ekoua and Koffi Adade have never allowed and never will allow their children to misbehave. At a very young age, we were exposed to very high moral, ethical, social, and educational values. It's fair to summarize the education we received from our parents in two words: sweet and sour.

Very few kids our age have experienced the kind of love and compassion our parents surrounded us with; by the same token, few of them experienced the kind of punishment we received from our loving parents.

Between my mom and dad, my father was tougher when it came to raising us. My mom, like many other mothers, in many occasions allowed the gentleness of her feelings to influence her when it came to punishing us. On many occasions, she would yell very loud with her always "clear voice" without necessarily punishing us physically.

My dad, on the other hand, was the head of the family, the "number one" master of the household, and didn't hesitate on any occasion to prove it to us. Even though my statement judgment might sound harsh, we children easily understood why he was so tough while raising us. The point my father wanted to get across was that he loved us so much that he couldn't live with himself if he didn't raise us properly. Through his love, he wanted to make this strong statement: "Children, I wasn't lucky enough to have my own parents to raise me when I was a child. But you should be happy to have me as your father, for I'm ready to sacrifice myself to make sure you have me by your side whenever you need me." As my father always told us, "When I was a child, because I didn't have my own parents to raise me, I used to listen to the advice other parents gave their children to help educate myself. It was neither easy nor fun for me, kids."

Both my parents were very strict when it came to raising us; they love to say that the best time to make a plant take a desired shape is when the plant is still young enough to be flexible and adjust to change. Once that plant becomes a tree, it's too late; you'll have to leave it alone, or else you will break it.

Perhaps my parents liked this image because they were farmers. With this strong conviction, our parents didn't let us get away with any nonsense. One Friday evening, when I was about eleven, I set myself on a collision course with my mother. At the time, we were still living near my father's relatives in downtown Agadji.

My mom had just returned from the farm, which she always did around 5:00 p.m. to be sure dinner was ready by the time my father got home around 6:30 p.m. While I don't recall exactly how my trouble with my mother started that evening, I must have done something naughty, and so my mom spanked me a little.

As I was the troublemaker in the family, it wasn't unusual for my parents to spank me now and then more frequently than my siblings. I usually cried for about a couple of minutes, most of the time with dry eyes, and then I'd be quiet for a while until I found myself in hot water again. That evening was unusual; my crying went on and on, seeming to be unending. I think my empty stomach added fuel to the fire of frustration and unhappiness that was burning inside me that evening. Our fellow villagers, who watched me as I was growing up, can attest to the fact that "Pierre did not like to have an empty tummy."

So that evening, around six, after my mother had taken time away from cooking dinner to spank me a little, I was a little hungry and unhappy. My weeping went on and on to the point where my mother was getting frustrated. After warning me several times to be quiet, she decided to give me another dose of spanking, stronger this time.

Even though I was crying, I was on guard because I was suspicious of what my mother's next move would be. So I was ready when my mother, moving quickly and intelligently as wild animals do in the jungle to capture their prey, tried to catch me again. This time, with the Lord's blessing, I managed to escape and started to cry louder, the same way any bad boy will do.

During my escape, I dared talk back to my mom, several times shouting and crying, "Leave me alone!" My mother was not pleased. In my agitated state, I had violated a very important taboo in my parents' home—never talk back to elders, especially parents. Well, on top of that, the fact that I was crying louder, making my mother look like a bad mother who was abusing her child in front of our neighbors, breaking one of the most sacred laws in our house, really set my mother off.

Through my tears, I could see my mother was really mad at me, but she swallowed her anger, turned away from me, and went back to cooking dinner. It was getting dark, so I hid a few meters from the kitchen in the shadow of our grain silo. By the tine dinner was ready, my father had returned from his farm.

My toughness started melting away as I started getting scared; I knew what my father's reaction would be after my mom reported my behavior to him. Also, I started getting scared of the thick blanket of darkness that was beginning to cover the village. While I was feeling vulnerable, my parents decided to strike.

My parents asked my older brother Fidel to locate where I was hiding, sneak behind me, and make sure that I didn't escape this time around. My parents' plan of action worked, and before I knew it, I was caught. Now I felt as weak as a baby. Even though they had me, my parents decided not to spoil my dinner by disciplining me right as soon as I was captured. For my parents, dinnertime was too sacred to be spoiled.

*****

Dinnertime was indeed special. It was a time for sharing ideas and, more importantly, for learning how to behave. While my mother and my female siblings shared their meal together seated on the kitchen floor, my father, Fidel, and myself ate in my father's living room or on night of the full moon outside. We ate seated at a forty-five-by-thirty-five-inch wooden table. Before eating, we all washed our hands with soapy water and rinsed them. Dad always said a prayer, usually an Our Father and a Hail Mary, and made sure Fidel and I said them with him. Only then could we eat.

We were allowed to sit on the chair during dinner. While we had some privileges, there were also some taboos. We were not allowed to burp loudly, talk while eating, or make funny noises while chewing the food. Especially forbidden was eating meat from the sauce until our father gave it to us, which usually would only happen toward the end of the meal.

We were also supposed to learn to eat slowly or at least not faster than our father. During a meal, if Fidel or myself happened to say, "I'm full," before our dad was done, he would order us to stand on the table with our arms crossed on our chests until he declared dinner formally over.

After dinner, either Fidel or myself would bring in soapy water to wash our hands again, while the other bussed the table and took the dishes to the kitchen.

While Fidel and I had more privileges than the female members of our family at dinnertime, I strongly believe that they spent the meal in a special manner in the kitchen but in a less formal, more relaxed manner.

*****

Usually on Fridays and Saturdays, when dinner was over, we children were allowed to go to bed early if we chose to. We were released from our Monday-through-Thursday routine of having to study prior to bedtime on Fridays and Saturdays because those two night were reserved for weekend pleasure time.

As a child, my favorite weekends were during the full moons of the dry season. When the moon was full and the whole village was shining and beautiful, we were allowed to go out and play games, such as hide-and-seek, with our neighbors. Once in a while, our parents would come out and watch us play. Around 10:00 p.m., from all directions, the village was filled with the voices of parents calling their children to return home and go to bed.

*****

That night, I got into trouble; there was no trace of moon in the sky. It was very dark out, so though it was a Friday night, we did not have the luxury of playing outside. I went to bed early that night with the feeling that my trouble was not over, even though my parents hadn't given me any impression that they were holding anything against me. That night, I had a good sleep, for as we say in my Akposso tribe, "One should not refuse to go to sleep for fear that he might not wake up again"—a small comfort for me, knowing that I probably would be punished in the morning.

About five that next Saturday morning, I was awakened by my father. Now I was going to get it. I was invited to the living room where both my parents and my siblings were waiting for me. Pauline, Fidel, and Jeanne were half asleep, and I guessed they were there more as witnesses of my cunning punishment than as jurors. The trial didn't last long. I was found guilty with the most serious charges being disobedient to my mother and, worst of all, talking back to her. The sentence—a major whipping—was to be carried out in the early morning to avoid the neighbors trying to intervene.

*****

Pauline, being the oldest child, took the most heat from our parents, especially our father. He raised her with an iron fist. Her teenage years were the most painful for her. She was allowed to socialize only with female friends. Her movements outside our home were strictly supervised by my father's spying eyes.

Due to my mother's influence, at age fifteen, Pauline was allowed to have a little taste of freedom by joining a Youth for Christ group called CV AV, in French "Cœurs Vaillants-Âmes Vaillantes."

This Christian group, similar to scouting groups in the United States, was under the command of a very popular elementary school teacher named Mr. Akpossogna Martin, widely known in my village as Teacher Akpossogna. The group was the most popular and active during the '60s and '70s. Youngsters ranging from seven to thirty were allowed to join CV AV. This group performed a wide variety of activities. They sung during Sunday services in a junior choir and performed plays about the Nativity of Jesus Christ during the Christmas season and the Passover during the Easter season.

One of my favorite plays that the CV AV performed was an original play about two guys who got rich by taking advantage of good Samaritans in a very dishonest way. These two guys were named Otar and Capito. These two got up one morning and traveled twenty miles away from their own village into an area where they would be strangers to the inhabitants.

The plan was that they would stand on the side of the main path and wait. As soon as they heard a human voice approaching, one would lie on the ground and pretend he was dead. The other would start crying his eyes out. They would continue the charade until the "good Samaritan" villager came up to them to see what the matter was.

Capito agreed to be the first to lie down. As soon as they heard a potential good Samaritan approaching. Otar started his tearful wailing over his "dead" brother. As predicted, the unsuspecting villager was concerned.

"What has happened to your brother?" the good Samaritan asked.

"It's really a sad story. I don't know how to explain," sobbed Otar. He continued between faked cries, "My dear brother and I were on our way to visit some relatives when all of sudden he started having chest pain. Before I could do anything to assist him, my dear brother dropped dead."

"What a pity!" the good Samaritan acknowledged. "How can I be of assistance?"

"You know," Otar continued, "the saddest part of all this is that I don't have even the first penny to have my brother transported back home." Otar continued his false tears until the Samaritan started talking again.

"Well," the Samaritan said, "I really don't have much money on me today, but here are two hundreds francs to help you take your brother back to your family. I'm really in a hurry, and I have to go now. I'm sorry about what happened to your brother."

"Thank you very much, and may God bless you," Otar gushed. As soon as the Samaritan disappeared, Capito jumped up laughing, proud of their malicious trick.

"Two hundred francs! That is a lot of money, isn't it?" asked Otar.

"Of course!" responded Capito. "Let's do it one more time. This time, you be dead, and I'll do the crying."

"Okay, okay." Otar smirked, rubbing his greedy hands together.

A few minutes later, they heard two men coming. Before they noticed Otar and Capito, Otar took his cue and dropped dead. At the same moment, Capito started crying. They were sure their plan would work, but this time, they would be surprised. These two men were more than potential good Samaritans—they were a priest and his assistant. As they got close to the "dead" body, Capito started using the same sorry words Otar used earlier to get sympathy and money.

"We are really sorry to bear this. Unfortunately, my assistant and I are priests and don't have any money to give you to transport your brother back home. We can help by blessing your dear brother so that the good Lord in heaven will accept him into His Paradise. We can also help you bury your brother right here so you won't have to worry about taking him home."

When the priests made this unwanted offer, Capito panicked. "No!" he protested. "I must take my brother home. He cannot be buried in a foreign land!"

"My son," the senior priest insisted, "all this land, including your native land, belongs to the same God, and since, we all are children of that same God, it does not make any difference whatsoever where you bury your dear brother."

Nearby was a deep hole that resembled an old tomb. The priest and his assistant decided to bury Otar in there, and while they were busy arranging the tomb, Capito knelt next to his friend, as if he was still crying, and whispered, "Listen to me now, Otar. This is no longer funny. These two priests are determined to bury you. We have to do something really fast, or you'll be buried alive."

"Here is my plan. You wait until the priests and I lift you up from the ground, and as we are getting close to the tomb, I'm going to make a noise. At the noise, you will open your eyes. They'll be frightened, and we'll run away. Understand?"

Poor Otar, frightened almost to death, was delighted that his friend had come up with an escape plan. He also had no other choice but to agree.

The priests came back. As the dead body was being transported to the tomb, Capito made his noise signal. Otar opened his eyes suddenly and started moaning.

Terrified by this unexpected event, the priests dropped Otar and ran away as fast as they could. Capito also ran away though in a different direction.

Otar and his buddy reunited a few minutes later and hurriedly returned to their hometown two hundred francs richer but promising each other not to try their scheme again.

*****

In addition to their performances, the CV AV did volunteer work such as helping the poor, the elderly, the ill, or the handicapped in the village. The members would supply these people with drinking water from the creek, firewood for their kitchens, and even money to buy food.

This CV AV group in which all four of us siblings at one point all participated in, helped us learn our strong social and moral values. It also helped every member, including Pauline, to blossom out of a teenager's shyness and to learn to publicly express her opinions.

My father didn't have any problem with Pauline joining CV AV because the group met in the early evening and because Pauline went to the meetings with her female friends and cousins. Even if the meeting happened to last longer than usual, it always ended before my father got too nervous.

However, my father did have a problem with the dancing parties that were organized by the young men of the village, who ranged in age from teenagers to men in their early thirties. These dances usually occurred around Christmas and Easter. There is neither a specified drinking age nor legal curfew for parties in my country. During those parties, which didn't start until 9:00 p.m., youngsters, hot as they were, would dance and drink all night, some of them getting pretty drunk, which often led to things happening that did make any concerned parent like my father very nervous.

The atmosphere of joy and euphoria around Christmas and Easter pushes some men and women to act silly. Because alcohol, including beer, wine and Sodabi, is legally served at parties during those holidays and because the parties last all night, young men and women find space to become romantically and sexually involved without necessarily giving it much thought. After all, they think it's holiday time—time to celebrate, time to enjoy life, and life is too short. Some unlucky women get pregnant during these celebrations—a fate my parents did not wish for their oldest daughter.

My father had a serious problem with all that heavy partying. While my dad understood that his daughter Pauline needed to enjoy her youth, he was not ready to watch her jeopardize it. My dad was not ready to let his firstborn daughter spoil her youth because of some stupid and regretful act. So Christmas and Easter times scared my dad the most. He felt the obligation to let Pauline go and enjoy herself with her friends, yet he didn't want her to make any mistake. To help ease his own mind, my dad used to wait up for Pauline to get home before he went to bed. He might fall asleep in the living room waiting, but that didn't matter to him. He would never go to bed until Pauline had returned.

My father worried most during Pauline's teenage years. One Christmas Eve, my father forced Pauline to take her two brothers, Fidel and myself, with her to a party. Fidel was around thirteen, and I was around eleven. We were obviously being used by our dad as Pauline's bodyguards and his secret agents. Our dad also gave Pauline a curfew because he knew very well that after a certain time, Fidel and myself might fall asleep at the party. Then with his secret agents' eyes closed, anything might happen.

One Christmas Eve party that Pauline was forced to take Fidel and me to was so wonderful that Pauline violated her curfew by a few minutes. Fidel and I were still wide awake and watching when, to the astonishment of everybody, my dad showed up at the party to escort all of us, especially Pauline, home. Pauline was still on the floor dancing a slow dance with a young man from the village when my dad walked through the door. Seeing our father, Pauline stopped dancing before she had a serious heart failure. Most embarrassing of all was that Pauline had to leave the dance floor while the music was still playing. Thank God Pauline, knowing the kind of father she had, did not resist his summons. She never was stubborn or rebellious; she always abided by her parents' rules and decisions.

Luckily, Pauline was a "good girl" that night because my dad had hidden a stick under his clothes—a stick he would have used without hesitation to whip Pauline in front of everybody had she dared oppose his authority. He would have whipped Pauline until she felt very sorry for herself. My father does not play games. Still, her humiliation that night was so great that she might have tried for the very first time to oppose him, but she politely and wisely chose not to. Instead, she started crying like a little child.

Though my dad could be criticized for being rude to his daughter, he clearly was proud of himself for showing the entire village that he didn't want any young man messing with his daughter. His message that night was indeed loud and clear. After that night, every young man Pauline's age feared my dad and respected Pauline. My father never had to repeat that crazy act; that day he again made sure his name would be remembered in Agadji history.

As was the custom in our home, Pauline was not punished until the early morning following that party, even though she may have felt that the humiliation she had suffered was more than punishment enough. Pauline's punishment was followed by a long bitter argument between my dad and my mom, who, as usual, was trying her best to defend her child from our father. However, my father gained the upper hand and punished Pauline severely. My mom cried with

Pauline to console her as well as to express her own remorse over not being able to save her daughter from the punishment.

My older brother Fidel and myself had a relatively easy life with our parents. I'm sure this was related to the fact that, unlike our poor older sister Pauline, we were male. In my male-dominated society, parents give more freedom and privilege to males, I'm sorry to say. For instance, boys are free to go out and play until dark with their neighbors, while girls are ordered to be home often before dark, around 5:00 p.m., to help their mothers cook dinner or do other domestic chores.

In my family in particular, even though our sister Pauline was, and still is, the child closest to our father, our dad's "favorite," Fidel and I were allowed to do things that Pauline was not. We got away with things that Pauline would have gotten seriously punished for simply because of our position as the true heirs and future heads of the Adade family.

As in other families, all four of us children gave our parents a lot of headaches during our teenage years, especially after we had moved to our home in Megbeadzre. Unlike our home in the village where the whole family shared a two-bedroom house, in Megbeadzre, there were more rooms and space. As a result, after our move, Pauline was finally allowed to have her own room next to our parents'. Jeanne, our youngest sister, still very young, shared the bedroom with our parents.

Fidel and myself could have had separate rooms because there were two nice cozy efficiencies available right behind our parents' room. Instead, our dad decided to use one as a storage room, leaving Fidel and me to share the remaining one, hence, limiting our independent movements. I'm convinced that this was our dad's way of allowing us two boys some freedom but not so much that we could abuse.

This move did not prevent Fidel, and younger brother Pierre from enjoying our space. Mistakes our parents made without thinking much about its potential side effects were to teach us as siblings to get along, protect, defend, and, most of all, love one another. I call this a big mistake because by the time we had become teenagers, these social and moral values were deeply implanted in us that we had become the most unified siblings in our village. No one could attack one of us without fear of reprisal from the rest.

Fidel and I developed such a strong relationship that despite occasional small fights, we were very willing to cover for each other even against our own parents.

One of our father's biggest worries was that we would start dating and eventually get girls pregnant. This particular worry of our father was founded in the fact that such accidents were common in our village. He was also concerned because we were clearly one of the few well-behaved and well-respected families, a "role model" family that attracted everyone, villagers as well as foreigners, older people as well as younger ones, male friends and potential girlfriends. The vast majority of the most beautiful girls in Agadji, as well as in the surrounding villages, always had their eyes on Fidel and Pierre and vice versa. This chemistry was created by the positive reputation of our loving, hardworking parents themselves with their high moral standards. Yes, the Adade boys would be good catches.

Unfortunately for our parents, especially our father, there was nothing he could do about his worries. There is a French proverb that says, "le vin est tiré, il faut le boire," meaning "If the wine is already poured, you'll have to drink it." Our parents' own efforts put Fidel and me on the favored side of our community, on the positive side of those beautiful girls. Well, we didn't have any other choice but to chase them. Figuring out how to date girls while sharing an efficiency was not a big problem for Fidel and his younger brother Pierre to solve. Being the only two males in the family and only two years apart, we became so close that making room for one another when one had a date or a visit was no problem. This new way of life first started with Fidel, as he was older. He would sneak out at night on to parties and dance with his friends while our parents were asleep, while Pierre stayed home, too shy to even say hello to the girls.

On many occasions, when Fidel returned home around midnight with a female friend, he would wake me up to make room for them. I would get up and continue my sleep under a tree behind our quarters—in a safe place where no one, especially our parents, would catch me by surprise. I swear I used to hate it, but at the same time, I was ready to cover for my only brother at any cost. I was determined to show him and the whole world how faithful I was to our agreement to protect and defend each other even against our own parents.

When the visitation of his female friend was over, Fidel would find me most of the time deeply asleep in a very uncomfortable position somewhere near the house, wake me up, and send me back to our room while he escorted his date back to her home.

Sometimes, when I wasn't very sleepy, I would escort his dates with him, and then we would return to our home together. Anyone who knew Fidel and myself never hesitated to call us the Adade brothers; some people even compared us to twins because growing up, Fidel and I loved to wear the same clothes, and in many ways, we behaved like twins.

It wasn't long before I started following in my brother's footsteps. In the beginning, I resisted Fidel's attempts to take me to parties and balls. I used to think it was foolish for anyone to buy a ticket for dances or parties just to dance and have a good time instead of saving the money for more important things such as food, clothing, and shoes. My view was that not only was a person wasting money, but returning home broke and tired after partying all night was very foolish.

My idea of a good time was going to movies and plays or "concerts" as we called them in my village. I never thought anyone could have fun dancing. Ah, how little I knew of what I was missing. Once I finally got a taste of these activities, I liked them. Soon I was going out regularly with Fidel on Friday and Saturday nights and almost every night when school was in recess. We usually went to parties or clubs, saw movies or plays, chased girls, or some combination of the above.

When I would return home accompanied by a date, Fidel would do for me as I had done for him—disappear and make room so that I could have my temporary privacy. During this time of my life, I came to understand what I had been missing when I had refused to go out with my dear brother. I enjoyed going out and chasing girls so much that pretty soon I became sharper at it than my brother Fidel.

I quickly became more popular than him among the girls because, unlike my brother Fidel, I was more outgoing, aggressive, and charming—even if I do say so myself.

My brother and my night activities did not go unnoticed long by our parents. All the precautions we used trying to return home unnoticed by our parents fell apart one night. To our great surprise, we were told on by our dog, Qui sait or Qui sait l'avenir, meaning "who knows" or "who knows tomorrow." Qui Sait, who usually watched us return without making any noise that night, barked so loud and long that our father woke up and came out of his quarters, thinking the dog was barking at thieves. While Fidel and I could rely on each other, we learned that night that we couldn't trust Qui sait. That night, Fidel and Pierre got caught with both hands in the cookie jar.

During our teenage years, American Western movies, AKA Cowboys movies were so popular in our village that it was almost considered a sin to miss one, as they came around only once in a while. It was more acceptable to miss a Sunday mass because one could make it up by going the next Sunday.

Fidel and I had made a secret deal not to miss any Western movies, especially if the actors happened to be our all-time idols and movie stars, John Wayne and Rich Nelson, to whom we gave a French nickname of Beau Gars or Handsome. Well, that night, Fidel had taken me to one of our favorite Western movie, *Rio Bravo*, which was showing at the residence of Jean Paul Felder, the then French Catholic priest. It was as if we were sneaking back home late from the movie that Qui sait, our dog, woke our parents up by barking too much. We were caught. We had not gone out that night chasing girls, as we usually did, but we couldn't deny that we were out late without approval. It was obvious to our dad that we were no longer his innocent young boys, so the possibility of being innocent until proven guilty was not a consideration. We were found guilty on the spot and ordered immediately to our room. In our room, we became so concerned about what Father would do to us in the morning that we started blaming each other for causing the barking of Qui sait, with Qui sait meaning who knows, or who knows the future?

In the morning, instead of punishing us the way he would have done with our sisters, our father chose instead to scare us by telling us about the consequences that dating girls could lead us to. "Now that I know you sneak out at night after the household is sleeping," our father declared, "I just want to warn you that if either of my sons dares to get some poor girl pregnant, I will automatically stop supporting him." He paused for a few seconds to collect his thoughts and continued, "Also, that person will be out of my household and move to his own place with his pregnant girlfriend and the unborn baby. There is no way," our father boomed, "that I will support both you and your pregnant girlfriend, wife, or whatever you want to call her. There is no way! Do you hear me?"

Our immediate reaction was great relief that our worst nightmare—a whipping—wasn't going to happen. Being whipped by our father was indeed more than a nightmare; it was close to torture. We simply couldn't believe our ears that our father was only lecturing us. Pauline, our older sister, would never have gotten away so easy.

Our relief stopped short as we started thinking about our father's threat. The consequences that our sneaky acts might lead us to suddenly seemed so scary to Fidel and me that we decided to do something about it. Luckily for us at that time, the government of Togo was introducing sex education into the schools. This sex education gave us the tools to safely avoid unwanted pregnancies as well as sexually transmitted diseases. We learned, thank God, how to figure out the fertile and infertile times of a female's ovulation cycle. Fidel learned first and then, as a good brother, taught me how to count to avoid problems.

About the same time, the government also started campaigning for family planning in our country through an agency called Association Togolaise pour le Bien-Etre Familial (ATBEF), meaning Togolese Association for Family Wellbeing. The ATBEF distributed condoms and birth control pills to everyone ages fifteen and above. This government program, which occurred under the pressure of Western countries to control birth rates in Africa, gave Fidel and his younger brother Pierre the very effective tools we needed to avoid feeling the sting of Father's threat should we slip up.

Thanks to our preventative measures, we managed to keep our father from exacting his punishment on us, or perhaps he thinks that we were after all "innocents." Neither of us have ever gotten a girl pregnant by accident, nor have we ever suffered from any serious sexually transmitted diseases. We were so successful in using our knowledge that Fidel didn't have his firstborn son, Romeo, until October 20, 1994, at the ripe old age of thirty-three, and his brother Pierre who left Togo to pursue his studies in Kalamazoo. Michigan still doesn't have any kids at the age of thirty-one.

*****

During his teenage years, Fidel got into major fights with my parents, actually with the whole family, including myself, when he started smoking Marlboros. Fidel always had a thing for the USA, and because Marlboros were manufactured in the States by Americans, he thought it was very cool to smoke "Marborros." Fidel's smoking bothered our parents very much; neither of them indulged in such vices. Our mother drinks only rarely, and our father does not drink at all. Neither of our parents smoke. In fact, before Fidel, no one in the Adade family had ever smoked. It came as a great shock to the family when we found out that Fidel had decided to become a volcano.

When he first started his new misadventure, he would only smoke with his friends and later as he grew bolder in front of me. Even though I categorically opposed Fidel's bad habit and uncharacteristically refused to follow in his footsteps, I did help keep his smoking secret from our parents. They didn't find out until our father caught him. My dad was furious and he took strong measures, including stopping Fidel's pocket money and giving him less money to buy food at school. Unfortunately, none of these measures worked.

By the time Fidel was caught by our dad, he was already somewhat addicted to smoking. Fidel kept smoking more and more, and sometimes when he didn't have any more money to buy cigarettes, he got money from me. I gave him cigarette money against my will, and for only one reason—to keep our brotherly relationship strong.

Our dad would have gone crazy had he found out that I was secretly supporting my brother Fidel with my father's money.

Father was by far the most furious about Fidel's smoking habit because he knew how bad cigarettes were for Fidel's health. One of his own cousins had died of lung problems caused by smoking too much. Another cousin, who was still alive and who was the one that my father had started his experimental coffee farm with, was losing his health because of smoking. Our father was more convinced than some doctors that smoking was bad for his son's health.

Fidel smoked for more than five years until he got tired of it and just quit in the early '80s. We had become convinced that Fidel would never stop smoking, not after five long years. As a united family, we accepted our differences and had eventually gotten used to Fidel's smelly habit. We had even stopped treating him like an outcast. Fidel's decision to stop smoking caught everyone in the family by surprise, including my father, but this time a very pleasant one.

Our younger sister Jeanne, unlike Pauline, had a relatively easy time of it with our parents. Jeanne was rather spoiled, being the last child born into our family and being the second and last girl. Her childhood was rosy. By the time Jeanne became a teenager, our parents, especially our father, had mellowed out; his attitude toward stubborn teenager behavior was more tolerant.

Jeanne was also lucky to have had an older sister and two older brothers who smoothed the way for her. By the time she became a teenager, Pauline, Fidel, and I were also old enough to oppose our dad when he was about to take his usual tough stand against her social activities. Unlike Pauline, who was very shy and quiet, Jeanne was very energetic, outgoing, and stubborn. Her character sent a clear signal to our father that he was dealing with a totally different daughter this time around, a different personality.

At a very young age, Jeanne had more freedom than Pauline had had. As with the rest of us, she was allowed to join the CV AV group in which she eventually became one of the leaders just as Pauline and myself had been. My parents' somewhat softened attitude toward Jeanne did not prevent them from punishing her just as they had every one of us if she crossed the line. They also taught her the same social and moral values they had taught her older siblings.

In fact, religious, moral, and social values, along with a school education, were the aspects of life that our parents valued most while raising all of us. Even though social values are the cornerstone of all African communities, my family's social life was rather limited. Though we were allowed to participate in many social activities, our parents drew a clear line for us as far as what we could and what we could not do. For instance, in my village, it's common to see a group of kids playing together at one of the group's house and often eating together when meal time comes around.

The parents of the host kid cook enough food for everybody. Many times I watched our mother doing exactly the same thing when we had friends over; the funny part of this was that we were strictly forbidden to eat at our friends' houses.

No matter how hungry we were, we could only eat at home. To any invitation to eat, Pauline, Fidel, Pierre, and Jeanne had the same answer, "No, I'm full, thank you." Even when we happened to be hungry, the answer was always the same. This was one of our parents' laws. We were so terrorized by the thought of the punishment that would surely follow our misbehavior that we found it easier to lie, saying we were full rather than risk eating at our friends' houses.

The only exception, the only place in the entire village where it was okay for us to eat beside our home, was at our grandma's (our mom's mother) and at our aunts' (our dad's sisters) homes in Amlame village, and we only went there on rare occasions.

In fact, our parents never ever left us at home without making sure we had enough food in the house to eat, which was not the case in some of our friends' households. We had no reason for eating elsewhere while we had food at home. We were taught to always come home to find something to eat whenever we were playing at our friends' house, and we were often hungry. We were taught to leave our friends' houses at least temporarily as mealtime was approaching to avoid the temptation of ending up eating there.

The lesson we learned from this law was a very precious one, self-control, and everybody in Agadji can testify that we Adade children had it. Time after time, we heard villagers saying, "Don't even bother to invite them to eat. Koffi and Ekoua's children don't eat at any place but at home." Other members of our family didn't like to hear that, but who cared? Not my parents; after all, it was good self-discipline and a family "law."

The truth of the matter was that the main objective of this strict law was not to be rude to our friends and their families; instead, in addition to teaching self-control, this rule was designed and strictly enforced by our parents to prevent us from harm. That the villagers all liked each other, there was no doubt, but my parents, unfortunately, had come to realize that we were surrounded both by people who truly liked us and by others who only pretended to. The latter were the ones that worried my parents. We children were too young to clearly identify who really liked us and who did not; we were too vulnerable. Our parents had the same problem, so they designed these tough rules to protect us as much as possible. My parents never forgot the two children they had lost, and while the cause of the death of the second child was still unknown, the first my parents knew had been killed by enemies of our family. As a result, my parents were not about to expose their living children or allow them to expose themselves to any unknown, potentially dangerous situation. Aren't we all afraid of the unknown? Well, my parents were no different.

Our parents never had any problem getting their rules or messages across to us not only because we were all good kids but also because we had learned at a very early age not to oppose them or cross their lines. The punishment that followed any serious misbehavior was always strictly enforced, well applied, and hard to forget. The punishments we received from our parents while growing up were so tough; today some people might be tempted to label them child abuse. They were not that. Our parents loved us too much to even think about abusing us. All of us were, and still are, very precious to our loving parents.

Whenever one of us did cross our parents' lines, they would not react right away. They might show their immediate reaction and their anger. Then they would pretend to have forgotten all about the incident until dawn the next morning. Around five in the morning, usually my dad would wake the violator up and invite that person to their living quarters, where my mother, half awake and shaking off sleep, was impatiently awaiting the beginning of the trial. My father was always the prosecuting attorney while my mom, bless her heart, always tried to cool the situation off a little, playing the role of defense attorney. Of course, my mom might join my dad in prosecuting. In those sad situations, the verdict was well known long before the end of the trial: guilty without parole.

As soon as the defendant arrived in our parents' living quarters, the questioning would start. Once begun, despite the early hour, it didn't take long before everybody, including the defendant, was wide awake. Depending on the circumstances, questioning could go on for as long as forty minutes before the guilty verdict was reached, as it was 99.9 percent of the time.

My parents never punished us until we were found guilty. However, once the guilty verdict had been reached, we all knew very well what would follow. My father, without any hesitation, would go into his bedroom and return with a solid and well-prepared stick or lash. What followed was always regretful, and it is needless to go into the specific details. It is enough to say that our parents, when it came to punishment, always gave us the "real thing" or the "full measure." The guilty one would be whipped until he or she forgot the difference between screaming and crying. When the whipping was over, the "cooling off time," which translates to our "release," occurred. We were forced to kneel on a bare floor for a half hour before being set free.

Sometimes, not only did we have to kneel but we were also ordered to stretch our arms out in front of us with elbows away from the body. In our hands were placed fairly heavy objects, usually rocks. Both arms were required to be horizontal to the floor with elbows straight. Next to the guilty one, one of our parents would stand. Most of the time it was—guess who?—my father, of course, making sure the punishment was well applied and the pains well felt. Did we hate those painful trial mornings? You bet!

Our parents always punished us at dawn so that no neighbors could intervene and try to rescue us. However, even if someone had tried, our parents would not have let anyone interfere, as it would supposedly only encourage our "bad conduct." During our trials and punishments, neither human rights nor child abuse organizations would have been allowed in our house; not even the closest relative was allowed to try to rescue us. Our parents' message was crystal clear: you cross the line, you pay the price. It was that simple.

We hated our parents during those painful brief moments, but when we reflected objectively on our punishment, we understood we had been wrong. Also, we knew that deep down in our parents' hearts, there was only great love, no hatred, no evil feelings toward us. Our parents loved and still love us all dearly, and we feel the same way toward them. Our love and respect for our parents always returned as soon as the pain from the punishment went away and was forgotten.

Looking back, my siblings and myself appreciate the value of those punishments; thanks to them we are what we are today. Of course, they were painful, but I also honestly think they were necessary evils.

In addition to spending time disciplining us, our parents devoted a lot of their very precious time to teach us morals. Growing up, our first and most important moral lesson was to stick together as a family. We were taught to view each other's enemies as well as each other's problems as our own. We were taught how to share everything we had with our siblings and then with others, if necessary.

Teaching us how to get along was one of our parents' toughest tasks. As in any family, there were a lot of animosities and fighting among us four children. We fought about everything. Sometimes, we fought for no reason at all. Maybe those fights were somehow motivated by our animal instinct to maintain territorial boundaries perhaps in response to the encouragement to share everything, and the fights occurred no matter how much we loved to share.

While Pauline and Fidel got along well with each other due to their shy and peaceful natures, Fidel and myself fought a lot, especially between the ages of ten up to our teenage years. We fought so often and so hard, especially during our parents' absence, that they started worrying that Fidel and I would never get along as brothers.

While our father was determined to force both Fidel and me to get along, our mother was discouraged by our attitude despite frequent reassurances from neighbors that we would eventually get along fine.

The relationship between Fidel and me did not only consist of fights. As predicted by neighbors, we eventually started appreciating each other and we simply put our animosities behind us and started getting along. When we fought, I have to admit that most of the time, I was the troublemaker, and when I finally stopped causing trouble, Fidel was able to get closer to me and take care of me the way good older brothers do.

Regardless of how close Fidel and I became. I really don't remember playing much with him while growing up in our leisure times, because of the two-year age difference, Fidel spent his leisure time with his older age group friends around the neighborhood, and I did the same with my younger friends.

We did do some things together; for instance, we took showers together and went to school together. During the 10:00 a.m. break, Fidel always came to my classroom and took me to the place where food was sold to school kids on the school compound. He would buy rice and tomato sauce for us to eat with the money our parents had given us. When break was over, Fidel escorted me back to my classroom before returning to his. Pauline had behaved exactly the same way with Fidel when he had been my age.

At noon, when school was out for the nap recess, Fidel returned to my classroom and took me home and then back at 2:00 p.m. when classes resumed. Then at 5:00 p.m., when school was out for the day, we returned home together. Sometimes Pauline came with us, but most of the time, she walked with her female classmates and friends.

On Sundays, we went to church either with Pauline, Mom or Dad, or by ourselves because the St. Augustine Church in our village was not far from our home.

Fidel and I loved to dress the same. We loved wearing the same things from our hair to our toes. Some villagers who were admirers of my family said we two were "fine," meaning "beautiful, nice-looking kids." Our haircuts were the same. They were also the same as our father's. The style was an imprint our father's life in Ghana had left on him. He always had his own hair cut the way people in Ghana did with beautiful lines, and on special occasions such as holidays, our father made the Ghanaian style lines in Fidel's and my hair—a fashion we went crazy for when we were growing up. Boy oh boy, Fidel and I loved those lines drawn in our hair, especially when they were handmade by our dad with his own comb. We knew we looked cute with them, but above all, we loved those lines because they made us look different from other kids and, therefore, very special. Like other kids, we loved being treated in very special ways, and our parents somehow managed to show us a special love without spoiling us too much.

Twice a year, after Mass on Christmas and on Easter, our parents took us four children to the only photographer in the village. We always had our pictures taken first with all four siblings together and then by gender, with Pauline and Jeanne together and then with just Fidel and myself. When our dad felt like spending more money on photos, he made us each have our pictures taken individually as well. Growing up, we had our pictures taken on a more regular basis than any other kids our age, and our photographers, first Mr. Alphonse Agbelekoussi and later Mr. Agbetome, will confirm that.

On those special occasions, Fidel and I got along very well until I would cause problems, usually after we arrived back home. I had to wait till we got home because we were taught never to fight or argue outside our home.

Our oldest sister, Pauline, was the calmest, shyest member of the family. Starting day one, she was taught to love and take good care of her siblings, and from that day on, Pauline assumed her responsibility with confidence, pride, and devotion. I don't remember Pauline ever hitting or insulting any one of us. At a very young age, Pauline amazed our neighbors by her self-control and, more importantly, by the quality of care she gave to her dear younger siblings, especially when our parents were away.

When she was in charge and we provoked her physically or taunted her verbally, Pauline always kept her calm, continuing in her role as the responsible older sister until our parents returned home;

then she would report to them, and they would give us the punishment we deserved.

My family, neighbors, and now deceased grandmother (our mom's mother) often retold one particularly touching story about Pauline.

In the late '60s, my mom had a health problem, and my father took her to an Italian missionaries' hospital in the city of Afagnan, about ninety miles from our village, where she would undergo stomach surgery. Pauline was eleven, Fidel nine, myself seven, and Jeanne five. The day prior to our parents' departure, we were placed in the care of our maternal grandmother who loved us dearly.

On our fifth day with our grandmother. I provoked an incident, which upset her. Though I can't remember exactly what I did, I do remember Grandma yelling at me until I started crying. My crying touched my dear older sister Pauline's little heart so painfully that not only did she try to console me with her own tears but she also decided right then and there to take us back to our own home.

Pauline waited calmly until our grandmother went grocery shopping. She then called for an emergency family meeting with her siblings. Pauline declared to our astonishment, "We are returning home now. I don't like that Grandmother yelled at Peter (as she called me). Hurry, pack your clothes and everything in this bag here. We are going back to our home."

Before we had any chance to voice our opinions, Pauline continued in tears, "If our parents were in town today, maybe Grandmom wouldn't have yelled at Peter the way she just did. Let's go now."

Ever the responsible one, before we left, Pauline made sure she locked our grandma's doors and left the keys in a safe place where she could easily find them upon her return.

When our grandma returned home from shopping, her home was empty. Her first reaction was to see whether we were at our home located only a short distance from hers. When she arrived at our home, it was dinnertime and Pauline had already started cooking.

Our grandma was so shocked and shaken that, for a few good minutes, she could not say a word. We thought she might have a heart attack, as she was so upset. When she was finally able to speak, she asked, "Pauline, why have you done this to me?" My grandma was very concerned that Pauline was just a little girl and was too young to realize the possible consequences of making such a decision, a decision that could easily ruin her ties to the family.

Without hesitation and for the first time, the usually calm and shy Pauline spoke out. Grandma tried in vain to make Pauline change her mind, but she was determined to protect her siblings at any cost. Grandma even appealed to us other three children, trying unsuccessfully to divide us and to get us to make our sister change her mind, but we were too attached to Pauline to let our dear sister down.

Grandma then started begging Pauline tearfully to change her mind, but she wouldn't budge an inch. Grandma even sought the intervention of our neighbors to soften Pauline's position, but her answer became an even more determined, resounding *no*. Finally, Grandma returned home in tears, sorrow, and humiliation.

For two long weeks, our eleven-year-old sister, Pauline, played the part of both our mom and dad. She cared for us with courage and determination. We did everything together. We took showers together, ate together, went to school together, studied, laughed together, and cried together.

Every morning before we went to school and evening before we went to bed, our heartbroken grandmother would come to spend some time with us. When we had time, we all went to visit her, but we always returned to our home sweet home.

For two long weeks, we tasted the life of parentless children; we really felt like orphans and we cried often, missing our beloved parents. The uncertainty of what was happening to our mother scared us almost to death, but as the disciples of Jesus Christ did after his death, we stuck by one another in our poor little home and prayed. We prayed our mother's surgery would go well. We prayed for her to get well soon so she and our father could return home to us. We prayed and prayed until the Almighty God heard our little voices. I was still a child, but I remember very well that day our parents returned home from the hospital.

It was a Sunday afternoon. We children were visiting our aunt, our mom's older sister, who was married and living in Amlame, a neighboring village five miles away. Our aunt's house was located both near International Road #2 and by the only creek near her house.

Fidel, some friend, and I were swimming in the Amutsi River when our sister Pauline came running and calling our names. We hurried out of the water, and Pauline, full of joy, quickly told us the very exciting news. Our parents were back from the hospital, and their cab was waiting with them inside to take us all back to Agadji.

This news brought us a lot of excitement. Not only were our parents back safe and sound, but we were also going back to our village in a taxi. In those days, and even today, cars are big luxuries, and we kids especially loved cars.

Upon returning home, our parents received two very different versions of what had happened while they were gone. The first version, of course, came from our grandma and the second version from Pauline and Fidel. Naturally, our parents were very surprised by Pauline's action of moving us back home, but clearly, they were proud of her courage and her endearing sense of love for her siblings, and they were proudest of her sense of responsibility. At the same time, our parents were not upset with our grandmother.

Both parents knew that our grandmother loved us dearly and were certain that she had meant well when she yelled at me. Luckily, this incident caused by me, Pierre, didn't spoil our relationship with our grandmother; instead, our family ties became even stronger and continued to be cherished by us until our grandmother passed away in 1986 at the age of sixty-five.

We all loved our grandmother not only because she loved us in return and was a loving person but because she was the only grandparent we ever knew. Our mom's father and our father's parents had died before any of us children had been born. In that fact alone were we less fortunate than other children who grew up surrounded by living grandparents.

In Africa, in my country, and particularly in my Akposso tribe, it's always a pleasure to have grandparents around. We learn so many good things from people of older generations, so we love to see them live as long as possible. In Africa, an elderly person who dies is thought of like a library that has been burned down.

*****

Word of the incident between our grandma and us children reached everybody in our own village of Agadji as well as those in the surrounding villages. Like thunder, it sent a clear signal to everybody that our little Adade family was not to be messed with by anybody—we were well known as being strong-willed and independent. To this day, the combination of our own good behavior and our parents' makes our family one of the most feared and respected in the area.

Another unhealthy fight in my family occurred between Jeanne, our younger sister, and myself. Jeanne and I hated each other while we were growing up, and it was obvious I enjoyed fighting with her because I felt she was clearly being spoiled by our parents. I felt that my parents thought Jeanne never did anything wrong, and she always got what she wanted. I hated Jeanne because as a child, I was jealous—all the privileges I had to watch her enjoy had been mine. Ever since her birth, I felt that my parents had turned their attentions away from me and toward her. I hated that.

Jeanne soon realized that the main reason her older brother Pierre didn't like her was because of his jealousy. Unfortunately, to make matters worse, Jeanne decided in exchange to be obnoxious and to irritate me. As jealous as I was, I found myself with no option but to "show her my muscles"—the biological difference between an older brother and a younger sister. Unfortunately, usually Pauline, Fidel, or both were usually around to protect and defend Jeanne. I did not like that either.

The few times that I did manage to show Jeanne that I was a superman were when we were left alone together. On those occasions, if she dared look for trouble, she always paid the price, and I was then happy—happy to have finally proven to her that I was stronger.

However, my pride only lasted until our parents returned. Then Jeanne would dramatically describe what had happened between us while they were gone. Our parents would analyze the situation and react accordingly. In the majority of cases, whether Jeanne was right or wrong, if I had touched her, I was punished. By punishing me, our parents hoped I would learn to have the same self-control that Pauline and Fidel had. Learning self-control was very hard for me, as I loved to get even with Jeanne. I was different from Pauline and Fidel, but our parents refused to look at things my way. I didn't like that either.

In part, I was punished because none of us children was allowed to take justice into our own hands. Our parents preferred that one kept calm and reported problems to them; it was up to them to decide who was guilty and who was to be punished. However, my jealousy toward Jeanne, made worse by her provocations, made it difficult for me to keep my cool and always got me into trouble. To make matters worse, Jeanne enjoyed watching me being punished by our parents.

As in many families, Jeanne and I eventually became good and peaceful siblings as Fidel and Pauline were. Thanks to our parents' devotion to our well-being, over the years, we four siblings have built a very solid relationship that to this day marks the four of us as the closest group of siblings and family in our village, and anybody who has had an opportunity to meet the Adade family will agree.

*****

My parents have lived a happy life not because they are wealthy, they are not, but because they were fortunate to have four healthy children. By raising their children the right way, they have managed to show the entire village their philosophy of life and, above all, their ability to be good parents.

The only regret that both my parents have had is that they are illiterate. My parents, especially my father, still has bitter memories about his childhood and not having had the chance to go to school. Even though my father managed to become a very successful farmer, he thinks his community, his country, would have been better served had he been given the chance to be educated.

Though my father cannot predict what he could have done had he been educated, my honest guess, knowing my father, is that he could have been one of the finest lawyers my country has ever known. He could also have been a good accountant, for my father has an acute sense of statistics, the ability to save money, and healthy ideas about money management. He could also have been a good businessman because of his good investment ideas. My father could even have been a sharp politician, for he is a very wise and outspoken person. My father is well aware of all these hidden talents; unfortunately, he has never had the chance, as some others have been, to utilize them. Convinced that it is useless to feel sorry about roads he did not take, my father looks at the positive side of his life. My dad is also convinced that he has found as much happiness in watching his children go to school as if he had gone himself.

Even before my dad was married and had children, he was determined to do whatever it would take to give his children a chance to be educated. Unlike many parents in my village who didn't care much about sending their children to school, a school education was the number two priority on my parent agenda with a solid "home education" being number one.

My parents, unlike some, understood that all education must begin at home; thus, they raised us with a mixture of love and an iron fist—both essential to prepare us to accept, obey, and, above all, respect our society's rules, including respecting our elders. In addition, we were taught to respect all religious institutions whether they be Catholicism, Protestantism, or Islam, as well as political institutions, such as democracy, communism, and socialism. Our parents' greatest hope was to prepare their children well, the way a good farmer prepares his soil to nurture the seeds into healthy productive crops.

In a polygamist society like mine, where many parents ignore the education of their often too many children in part because of the very high cost of schooling in our country, my parents were among the few who were more than ready and willing to devote themselves hundred percent to the future well-being of their children.

Despite all the difficulties of farming life, my father earns a sufficient yearly income from his coffee farm to live a somewhat comfortable life. He earns roughly $2,000 a year. In my village, where the average person makes about one-fifth of what my father makes, he is considered one of the very few farmers who is better off financially. Even though my father could by no means qualify as wealthy, he could have afforded to have certain luxuries, for example, to have electricity put in our home or to buy a used car or a color TV set. Instead, he and my mother decided to spend their earnings on our education.

Our parents never tried to hide their own illiteracy. However, they reacted differently to our getting an education. Our father involved himself with us and was always eager to learn, so eager that he would bug us children all the time to teach him how to say "such and such" in French, and he always had us share with him the lessons we had learned that day at school.

Our mother, though very outgoing and very warm by nature, was very shy when it came to learning from us. Her weapon of defense was that she didn't need to know French to be happy or to survive. "You guys do," she would say.

*****

In my village, my parents are well known for putting education of their children on the very top list of their agenda. We felt their support in every detail of our school life, and that support was free of the pressures and expectations many of our classmates lived under.

In a community like mine where the rate of illiteracy is very high, parents often invest in their children as a means to secure their old age. An African child is like a social security card to his/her parents, especially when this child becomes well educated and eventually holds down a nice job. This child, make no mistake about it, becomes guaranteed security for the entire family. Even parents who don't devote any time to helping their children succeed in life find ways to reap benefits from them.

Unlike those parents, my dad didn't want us to feel pressured or under a moral obligation to take care of him. He wanted us to understand that his help to us was hundred percent free of charge, even tax-free, to understand that his help was motivated by the one and only true feeling of *love*. As he always said, "I'm a fighter. I know how to take care of myself. I will know how to survive. Once I'm done helping you succeed in life, I will then start saving for my old age, so don't you worry about me."

Growing up, we listened to statements of this nature from our father—statements that often were as long as speeches. Anytime my father started talking about a topic that was dear to him, the listener could expect him to go on for a long while before even a short break. Yes, anyone who knows my father will agree that he loves to talk.

I will never, ever forget the touching, emotional statement our father used to whisper in our ears as we were growing up. "I would rather sacrifice everything I have, even go naked and see you, my children, succeed in life than spend the little money I have on personal luxuries and deny you an education. As you well know, when I was your age, I wasn't fortunate enough to have someone there to back me up for an education. Believe me, it hurts like an open wound. I do not wish for you to experience even one iota of what I've been endured. All I want from you is for you to take advantage of my willingness to help you, to build a secure future for yourself, as well as for the generations to come. You don't have to pay me back. You really don't even have to take care of me in my old age either. I don't expect any of these things from you. I just don't want any of you to look back years from now and blame me for not helping you to succeed in life. I just want you to be happy because I love you."

Our father was always very diplomatic and careful in his statements. He spoke for himself and only for himself without including our mother, almost as if she didn't exist, and why? Simply out of fear that our mother might not agree with what he said. Our father also understood that a wife and husband, no matter how united they are as a couple, may have different ideas concerning their children. Though our mother always listened quietly to our father's statements as if she agreed with her husband, our dad respected and, to some extent, feared his wife's silence.

*****

School uniforms were one of our parents' first concerns for a long time. Every year, two or three weeks before school started, our parents were busy at their machines sewing our uniforms for the new school year. Our mother was in charge of Pauline's and later Jeanne's uniforms while our father took care of Fidel's and mine. This tradition continued for a long time until our parents' time became consumed by their farm activities and until we children were tired of wearing our eternally "special," homemade uniforms.

Despite the fact that schooling was expensive in our village, money was never an issue in our family. Our father was never late in paying our tuition. In fact, he was always one of the very first to pay. Our dad also was one of the first to buy their children school materials, such as reading and writing books, pens, pencils, and rulers. At the local Catholic bookstore run by the French missionaries, our father was a regular customer, and he always had enough money to cover the cost of our materials at the beginning of each school year because of his excellent financial planning.

During our elementary and junior high years, our parents hired tutors for us, not because we were stupid or slow but because they wanted to give us the extra push we needed to succeed in school. Every evening after dinner around seven, the tutors, high school students themselves, came to our home to assist us in doing our homework and to answer our questions concerning things we hadn't understood in class. Help was mostly needed in math, the natural sciences, and physics. The tutors also helped us with our writing and spelling. I am not sure how much money our father paid them, but I do know that our tutors all enjoyed working with us not only because we were well-behaved kids but also because we did well in school, personal proof to them that their efforts were bearing good fruit.

During the tutoring sessions in our dining room, our mother spent her time nearby doing dishes cleaning up the kitchen or relaxing, and our father locked himself in his bedroom. In his bedroom, our father seated himself right next to the closed bedroom door so close that he could hear everything the tutors were saying. He could also hear whether we children were paying attention to the tutors whether we were repeating after them. At the same time he was keeping an eye on us, our father was learning French. These tutors would have charged our dad extra fees had he told them that he was interested in learning himself. He was very clever. Behind his bedroom door, our father was not only learning French without disturbing us, but he was also keeping us alert because if we got caught playing around, we would be punished. Our father's eavesdropping behavior also kept the tutors on their toes.

Our father learned so much and so fast through listening to our lessons that very soon he became our "coach." He couldn't do the tutoring; after all, he didn't know more information than we did. What he did do was to drill us, especially with our spelling *dictee* in French (in English "dictation"). He would hold the reading text and read in his broken French a couple of sentences, which we wrote down in our homework book. He then matched each word with those in the text to see which were spelled correctly and which were wrong. While we gained more knowledge from our tutors than we did from our dad, his message to us was a very clear one: he wanted us to succeed in school.

If my memory is correct, our father could very well have been the only villager and one of the very few farmers in the village who showed such motivation and determination regarding their children's school education. We didn't become, as a result of this personal devotion from our dad, the most brilliant kids in our classrooms, but we were not the dumbest either. Still, there is no denying that our parents' energy and help did make a big difference in our school education.

Our parents' support for our education extended to helping us get to school. When my brother Fidel and I entered junior high, our father bought us brand-new China-made Flying Pigeon bicycles. This at a time when the vast majority of the students, and even some teachers, walked to school. Riding a brand-new bicycle to school was a sign of great privilege. Our parents' intention was not to spoil Fidel and myself but to facilitate our movement and to discourage us from being late to class.

In addition to dressing us for school, paying our expenses, watching us study, and getting us to class, our father never missed a single parents' meeting. At these meetings, parents learned firsthand from the teachers how their children were doing in class. These meetings were also places where parents talked together and developed new ways of coaching their children at home.

One policy the parents came up with was not to let children go to bed before a certain hour, even if they were sleepy, until their assignments for the day had been completed. I vividly remember being powerless, as our father enforced this policy with an iron fist. We children were forced to stay at our study table until the lessons of the day had been memorized. Of course, the faster the lessons were learned, the earlier we were allowed to go to bed.

If one of us got caught sleeping during our study hours, 8:00 to 10:00 p.m., the offender was ordered to stand for ten good minutes until the sleepiness went away. Sometimes, we were ordered to go wash our faces with cold water when fatigue and sleep tried to take over our little bodies. Though all these techniques may seem appropriate, they were at the time worse than torture for us because it was very hard for us to chase away sleep once it had weakened our nervous system.

At times we grew sleepy earlier than others. The cause of our sleepiness was not important to our father. Whether we had eaten too much that evening or if we were just tired, he always got very upset if we fell asleep with our heads on the study tables.

When our mother dared intervene in our defense, he got into arguments with her, especially about how she was spoiling us. Our father hated the idea of spoiling his children, even though he did it himself without necessarily admitting it. He was afraid that if we became spoiled, we would stop being "role model" kids.

Finally, before we were permitted to go to bed, our dad himself verified if the lessons had been learned. He also checked our notebooks daily to see if we were getting good grades in school. Bad grades one day meant longer hours of study that evening; good grades were rewarded with extra pennies for lunch the next day.

*****

Education in my country, from first grade all the way to university level, is very tough, designed on the challenging French system that doesn't allow a student who wishes to succeed to fool around at all. This system, in fact, keeps students on their toes from the beginning to the very end. Unlike in the United States, where tests are often designed using true/false or multiple choice questions, the French system utilizes only essay questions. Students must write in a well written (good grammar and vocabulary) essay their complete knowledge on the question being asked. Regular quizzes and pop quizzes take place very often as well to constantly check the students' knowledge and to motivate them to participate in class.

At the end of each trimester, we students were submitted to a full week of tough exams—the first before Christmas recess, the second one before Easter recess, and the third at the end of June or beginning of July, depending on a student's class level. The first two sets of exams were just "tests," while the third determined who would move to the next level and who would repeat. Repeating a class meant spending a whole year at the same level, and this could happen over again until a student finally passed or dropped out.

On the last day of each trimester, before we left on recess, the local Catholic elementary school we attended held its traditional D-Day. On that day, students were notified of their grades by their teachers. The notification took place around 3:00 p.m. in a very public event. The student body, their parents, and everyone in the village were invited to come and see for themselves the students' results. This ceremony was designed to embarrass "bad" students, to excite them to work hard, and, more importantly, to reward the "good" students who had showed a lot of effort and commitment to their education.

During the ceremony, the ten best students of each level were given many rewards for their academic achievement, such as notebooks, nice pens, reading books, and candies; they also received a big applause from the assembled audience. Then students who managed to pass were also praised though on a lesser scale. Yes, it was a wonderful day for the "good" students. These students brought home with them joy and happiness for themselves as well as for their families.

Students who didn't get passing grades were by no means punished. Only on the rarest of occasions were the laziest students whipped in front of everyone, but the indirect humiliation they endured on those occasions in front of the eyes of the whole village, including their parents, was greater than any other possible punishment. The humiliation these "bad" students would spread to include their parents and families; this is one reason parents never liked their children to fail.

Like all students, we Adade children experienced successes and failures, happiness and shame during our school years. During my elementary school time, I failed twice and had to repeat the class, Cours Moyen Deuxieme Annee or CMII, the class required to move into junior high. I failed not because I wasn't smart enough but because at that time, the early part of my puberty, I was having too much fun at parties and going on dates when I should have been studying. I was being initiated into how to date girls by my older brother Fidel, assisted by some of my best and closest friends, including Antoine Kedjagni.

Pauline, Fidel, and Jeanne also experienced a time in their lives during which they failed some courses; in fact, they failed more often than I did. Although failing exams was tolerated in some families, this never was the case in my family. We children knew we would pay a price one way or another. Often when we failed, the punishment we received from our parents was more psychological than physical. We might be grounded for a week, deprived of leisure time, confined to longer hours of study, or worse, forced to wear our old clothes to church on a special holiday like Christmas or Easter when our friends were wearing their new ones.

This punishment was painful because like any other kids, we loved wearing new outfits, especially during the holidays. Yes, we loved to show off a little with our new clothes at church. Once or twice, our mom succeeded in convincing our dad to back off from his punishment by allowing us to wear new clothes during holidays regardless of our having passed or failed our exams. However, usually our dad was determined and our mom could not change his mind. Regardless of the punishments, we always had fun together as a very close family.

My parents not only believed in discipline to encourage us to follow their wishes and to succeed in school, but they also highly valued praise and rewards. When we passed our exams, we were given new clothes and new shoes to wear at the holiday seasons.

*****

After we had moved to our new home in Megbeadzre and our father had stopped hiring private tutors for us, he made another smart move. He rented a two-bedroom apartment of his to schoolteachers. He had rented to elementary teachers when we were in elementary school and then only to college professors as we went through junior high and high school. Our dad managed to build an unusually strong landlord-tenant relationship with all these teachers, and before we or they realized it, these poor teachers became his "secret agents" and our free tutors.

Our school years in junior high and high school were less embarrassing than those in elementary. Grades were no longer read in front of the entire village; instead, they were sent out individually and directly by first-class mail to parents.

As soon as we had finished our school exams, our dad started "bugging" us as to when our report cards or bulletins would arrive. Our father was always anxious to see our grades, so anxious that most of the time he forgot it took time for our teachers to grade our papers and put the bulletins together. Our father loved to see our grades. When Fidel and I did poorly, he used them as proof that we were sneaking out at night—proof that we were out chasing girls and not studying.

Not many days in my family were as tense and scary as those when our report cards arrived. That day was for us as scary as the original D-Day when Allied Forces landed in Normandy on that infamous day in World War II. On our D-Day, we knew our father, the judge, would submit us to preliminary hearings, trials, and sentencing all combined.

*****

Our father loved to ask us tons of questions on the school subjects we didn't do well in. He was more knowledgeable about the various subjects that we studied in class that most illiterate villagers and he was very concerned about our grades. We were expected to do well in all subjects. Our father wanted us to be as successful in our studies as he was as a farmer.

According to our father, a "good" student should be able to do well in every subject. He didn't understand the difference between mathematics, natural science, physics, chemistry, history, geography, French literature, English, or philosophy or why some students did better in math, for example, than others.

Unfortunately, the variety and complexities of the subjects we were studying did not allow us to be as good as our father was on his farms all the time. Like other students, we had our strengths and weaknesses. We had our favorite subjects, subjects we always did well in, as well as subjects in which we never got good grades no matter how hard we studied. These subjects always got us into big trouble with our dear father.

Our dad could not comprehend why Pauline, Jeanne, and I always got good grades in French, geography, history, biology, and geology and then turned around and got bad grades in math, physics, and chemistry, while my brother Fidel did just the opposite. He could not understand what was preventing us from getting good grades in all subjects. Well, we couldn't understand it either; therefore, when we were questioned about these things during our lengthy and boring hearings, we never gave our dad good answers. All we knew was that we studied each subject as hard as we could, and for some strange and mysterious reasons, we didn't pass some.

The only time the hearings were short was when we managed to come out with overall passing grades for the trimester; those passing grades resulted from the combination of all subjects studied. After all, it was the trimester's overall passing grades that really mattered, and our father was well aware of that.

Luckily, 90 percent of the time, we received overall passing grades, though we didn't necessarily pass each subject. It's simply true that some subjects were harder than others for each of us.

Though our father could not claim his children were as successful in school as he wanted us to be, he was clearly satisfied with our commitment to our education and our efforts to do well. Although our father also could not claim his children to be the smartest in our village, our loving parents knew that their children were some of the most well-behaved who also did well in school.

Our parents' determination to see us make it was not limited to succeeding only in our village's educational opportunities. During our junior high and high school years, our parents helped us move from city to city in search of a better education and good schools. Our parents sent us to some of the best known public and private schools in Togo.

During her freshman year in junior high, Pauline attended a Catholic school run by nuns called Collège Notre Dame des Apôtres in Atakpame, twenty-eight miles from our village. During her junior and senior years, she attended other well-known public schools.

Fidel, during his junior and senior years, attended three different schools, among them a private one called College Protestant Methodist D'aneho or Protestant College in Aneho, a city near the Atlantic Ocean, fifteen miles from Togo's capital city of Lome and sixty miles from Agadji, our village.

Jeanne, our younger sister, also attended more than two schools during her teenage years, among them College Protestant Methodist D'aneho where Fidel had gone. Of us four Adade children, I was the only one to attend two major private colleges. During my freshman year, I attended a public college in our village called Collège d'enseignement général or CEG, translated as General Teaching College. Following my failure of the national exam of Brevet d'Etude du Premier Cycle or BEPC, which would have allowed me to start my junior year, my parents sent me to a different college.

During the academic year of 1982–1983, I was sent to Aneho to attend College Protestant as Fidel had gone and later Jeanne would go. In Aneho, I was lucky to live with a US Peace Corps volunteer named Tom Buchanan. This turn in my fortune began in 1981 when Tom Buchanan joined the Peace Corps after tiring of his routine but well-paid job as a fundraiser for Kalamazoo College aka K. College, a good liberal arts college in Kalamazoo, Michigan.

Upon their arrival in Togo, the Peace Corps office sent new volunteers to a three-month training school where they learned basic French, Togo being a French-speaking country and some of the main local African languages. Though I had worked at many training schools as a servant, including the one that Tom Buchanan attended, I did not really get to know Tom until his training was over and he was sent to teach English in the junior high school of CEG I was attending.

The Peace Corps program, one of the US's best contributions to development efforts in Third World countries, helps the individual person in countries through a wide variety of programs, including the teaching of English as a foreign language (TOEFL) in schools.

Tom Buchanan, part of the TOEFL program, was sent to my village as an English teacher. Luckily, the house in which Tom lived was just across the street from our new home in Megbeadzre. It did not take long before Tom, Fidel, and myself became so close that our friendship expanded to include our entire family. During his Peace Corps years in Agadji, Togo, Tom Buchanan was more than just welcomed by our family; he was well taken care of and protected by all of us. In fact, Tom Buchanan is considered a full member of our Adade family. My parents refer to Tom as one of their sons, and since Tom was older than our older sister Pauline, he became their oldest son. Ask my parents for Tom's full name, and without hesitation, they will tell you that it's Tom Buchanan-Adade, and if you ask Tom, he will tell you that he, indeed, has a family in Togo, West Africa—the Adades.

My parents' decision to send me to a different college happily coincided with Tom's decision to spend his third and last year as a Peace Corps volunteer in another city. When my dad told Tom of his decision, Tom offered to take me with him to Aneho. Tom Buchanan chose Aneho because he loves the water and the city is located on the Atlantic Ocean. Not only does Tom love to swim, but he goes nuts over seafood. He would die for a meal of fresh fish, crab, or especially shrimp and oysters.

Tom had learned about the special beauty of Aneho during his frequent visits to a best friend, also a Peace Corps volunteer, Russell Tomlin. He and Tom had met during their training in Atakpame. The two were very different with Tom being very energetic and out-going and Russ reserved and shy, but they were both very nice and generous people. Peace Corps volunteers often travel around the country to visit their friends, maybe to help alleviate their home-sickness, and Russ had visited Tom in our village on many occasions.

While Russ didn't care much about the ocean, Tom was dying to live by the sea. Once his decision was made, Tom contacted Russ about the idea of switching places. Russ Tomlin, easygoing as he was, didn't resist the idea. In fact, Russ liked the idea for two reasons. First, he knew how spoiled Tom was by the Adade family, having had a chance to get close to our family. Russ realized if he moved to Agadji, the Adades would treat him just as they were treating his buddy Tom. He was convinced that in Agadj he would be in good hands. Second, Russ was having some serious problems with his wife, also a Peace Corps volunteer, and he needed a place to get away. Sadly, Russ' wife later divorced him.

Following their agreement to switch villages, Russ and Tom contacted the Peace Corps office in Lome, which helped them move. Tom moved to Anello in August of 1982.

My academic year in Aneho with Tom Buchanan was a total success. Not only was I spoiled by Tom but more importantly I finally passed my national BEPC exam at College Protestant in June 1983. Passing the BEPC allowed me to move in the next level, which we call in the French school system the lycee. I really don't know how to express my deep satisfaction about my Aneho experience. I sure did have a lot of fun in Anello, and I have a lot of good memories from that time, memories that are still fresh in my mind as I write these lines.

In Aneho, I remember going to church every Sunday at St. Peter's just across the street from the two-story home Tom and I were living in. Tom and I lived in a nice three-bedroom apartment on the home's first floor. Above us was Lynn Thomas, another English teacher and Peace Corps volunteer.

Tuesdays were Tom and my favorite day of the week; it was the day the local outdoor market was held. Tom would give me money to buy fresh fish, shrimps, and oysters. Tom was a good cook, famous among his fellow volunteers; he showed me what American seafood cuisine was all about by cooking very delicious meals. Yes, Chef Tom Buchanan-Adade sure knew how to use a frying pan. I still swallow tons of saliva as I recall those meals.

At the end of the school year of 1983, following Tom's return to the United States, my dad sent me to another private school "College St. Joseph," one of the most prestigious and expensive colleges in the entire country, located in the capital city of Lome. In Lome, I lived with my older sister Pauline and her husband Mr. Kouma Yaovi, then a sergeant in the Togolese Air Force. Once again my school year was successful.

During my second year in Lycee, the equivalent of being a freshman in a US college, two major events occurred. I decided to try living alone not that I didn't have a good time living with Pauline and her husband. It was wonderful. I just wanted to have my own space. I discussed the idea with my parents, and they agreed. Knowing that I would have to start paying my own rent, I decided to reduce my dad's expenses by transferring to a cheaper public school, the Lycée de Tokoin in Lome, four blocks from College St. Joseph and five miles from my new home.

Tuition at Lycée de Tokoin was four times lower than at College St Joseph. Despite its less expensive tuition, Lycée de Tokoin was, and still is, one of the most prestigious and respected public schools in all of Togo. Unfortunately, my school year at Lycée de Tokoin was a total failure. I took the *probatoire* national exam, also known as Baccalauréat Première Partie (BAC 1) or first part of tile *baccalauréat* and failed by a very slim margin. Please believe me, I didn't fail my BAC 1 because I didn't study hard enough. The BAC 1 exam is known in my country as the toughest exam, and one must pass it to have any hope of entering the university. It was deliberately made to be very difficult by the Department of Education to reduce the number of students who would be eligible to compete for the privilege of attending the university. This may sound strange, but in Togo, the government spends a lot of money on the university and its students because there is almost no tuition for attending. The idea is to reward those individuals who have made it through all the difficult challenges to the level of being able to enter the university. However, money and space are limited, so the government does everything it can to minimize the number of potential students. In Togo, we have only one university, the famous University of Benin or UB—not to be confused with the neighboring National University of Benin or NUB.

The national exams we take in school at each level from elementary and all the way to university are as tough and challenging as tests required in the United States for one to attend a graduate school. By making the exam for university so tough, the government slows down the growth in the number of potential employees. In other words, school exams are successfully used by Togo's Department of Education as an unquestionably powerful weapon to manipulate unemployment issues.

As a result, in developing countries like mine where university education is in its infancy, very few make it to the university level. Perhaps, only one student in a village with a population of two thousand will make it to the university, and sometimes not even a single student makes it for many consecutive years.

Being able to attend the university back home is more than a prestige; it's an honor for one's village, and above all, it's an honor for the student's family. Attending the University of Benin in my country is as high an honor as attending Yale or John Hopkins University in the United States or like attending the Sorbonne in France or Oxford in England.

Because of this reality, most students who are able to attend the university and eventually get a decent job are likely to have many people expecting financial help from them, including their entire family—parents, siblings, and close relatives—and sometimes the entire village. Because of that heavy potential future social and financial responsibilities hanging on each student's shoulders, undergraduates rarely attend graduate school. In fact, many stop short of graduation, dropping out of the university and starting to look for job in order to start "paying back" those who helped them or perhaps to start fulfilling their role as their families' "social security." Those who do graduate look for a job in the government. While their education gets them "through the door," none of them are guaranteed of getting a job. Each educated student holding a paying job in my country is like a family bank where relatives, close and distant, turn to in time of financial crises.

Having said this, it is easier to see how a student who fails the national exam cannot and should not be considered lazy. I was by no means lazy when I failed some of my school exams. I studied my heart out, but I failed my BAC 1 at Lycée de Tokoin at the end of the school years of 1984–1985. I was truly crushed, but we were taught by our lovely parents to always get up after falling down, I was not discouraged. My parents were not discouraged either; instead, the following year, they sent me back to College St. Joseph. My well-intentioned attempt to save my parents' money by going to the cheaper Lycée de Tokoin did not work out.

Upon my return to St. Joseph College, I could hardly wait for the end of tile 1985–1986 academic year to arrive. I knew I could show the whole world that I could do just the opposite of what my family's enemies had been planning for me with my family's tremendous support and with the blessings of the Almighty Good Lord who from the day of my birth until now has always been good to me. I passed my BAC 1 exam in June 1987.

In 1988, I finally entered the mighty University of Benin, the highly honorable UB. I was the only one from my entire village to cross the threshold or our national university that year. It was quite an accomplishment and truly an honor for my entire community, as well as specifically for the Adade family.

I fondly remember the countless visits our dad and mom paid me (in fact, to each of us) while I was away from home attending college in different cities. They were emotional visits. Our parents always brought with them "presents" of necessities and luxuries, including money, grains, and delicious fruits such as mangoes, pineapple, bananas, avocados, oranges, guavas, and sugarcane—all of which came from our mountain in the Akposso region, welcome reminders of home.

I remember crying at the bus or train station at the end of each sweet visit, afraid that perhaps I might be seeing them for the last time. Luckily, our living God has been kind and generous to us. Our lovely parents are still alive and in good health.

*****

There are no words to describe my parents' devotion and determination regarding all four of us children's education. Our parents stood 200 percent behind us through that very demanding and difficult period in each of our lives, and thank God we all did quite well. Even though neither Pauline, Fidel, nor Jeanne made it to the University of Benin as I did, we all are very proud to be educated, and I know our parents, especially our father, who pushed us to do our very best, are proud of us for having accomplished what they themselves had dreamed of doing in their own lives—becoming educated.

Our father gave us the financial aid we needed. He firmly stood by his words that he would rather "go naked and spend all his money on us" and see us get an education rather than spend that money on his personal luxuries. Our father did exactly what he promised, and I just don't know how to express my gratitude to him, nor do my dear siblings Pauline Fidel and Jeanne.

We don't know how in this world to express our gratitude to our mother either. Our dear mother gave us the moral strength and love that we really needed to succeed in school.

Looking back, I realized how fortunate we were to have had Mr. Koffi Nicolas Edoh Igneza Otio Alifa Adade and his dear wife, Akoua Elisabeth Agbave Doumessi-Adade, for parents.

*****

My freshman year at the University of Benin was successful. I was about to start my sophomore year when our forever friend and "older brother," Tom Buchanan-Adade, arranged for me to continue my education in the United States, specifically in Kalamazoo, Michigan.

*****

After Tom finished his time with Peace Corps, he landed a job working with the USO and was first assigned to Italy. In Italy, Tom, as the director of the USO, not only had to deal with the US and Italian governments but also had the unforgettable privilege and honor to deal with the Vatican and the world's most popular head of state, Pope John Paul II. On various occasions, Tom had meeting and some special photos taken with the Pope.

While in Italy, our brother Tom paid for Fidel's visit there and mine. I was there first in the summer of 1987 and Fidel in the summer of 1988. By good coincidence, Russ Tomlin, the Peace Corps volunteer from Togo, and his older sister, Jeanie Springman, were visiting Tom at the same time I was.

During my visit to Italy, we traveled throughout that great country and saw places such as Pisa and its leaning tower, Sienna, Lucca, Florence, Tivoli, and Gran Sasso d'Italia, as well as famous places in Rome, where Tom was based, like the Coliseum, the Catacombs, the site of St. Peter's crucifixion, the mighty St. Peter's Square with its amazing church, underneath which we saw the mummified bodies of popes who had served from St. Peter to the very famous Sistine Chapel, the Treve Fountain, and the Vatican Museum. May I also say that thanks to Tom's ability to make good friends, we also had the unique honor of being taken on a private tour deep inside the Vatican by one of the Pope's Swiss guards, who was a good friend of Tom's.

From my two weeks in Italy, I will never, ever forget two events. The first was shaking hands with Pope John Paul II during his monthly public meeting, which occurred the first Friday of every month. The second was watching the Pope speak from a window of his residence on a Sunday morning to the weekly crowd gathered in St. Peter's Square.

My brother Fidel and I visited Tom in Italy on separate occasions, and I know Fidel has his own wonderful, personal, and different memories about a country that I personally recommend everybody visit at least once in their lifetime.

It was during my visit with him in Italy, prior to Tom's transfer to Frankfort, Germany, that he let me know of his willingness to send me either to France or to the United States to continue my education. As is clear from my story, I chose to come to the States partly because it was Tom's home; therefore, chances were that I would be well taken care of by his family and friends if anything happened. I also wanted to speak English as fluently as I did French—a very useful skill to help me in my future. The biggest reason for deciding to go to the States is that, like many people in my country, with my brother Fidel as its number one fan, the United States was a dream country. Fidel, in fact, pushed me hard to choose the United States. He didn't have to push too hard; it was exactly where I wanted to go.

While Tom was living in Frankfort, Germany, he made the arrangements for me to go to the States. It all came together in June 1989 when Tom Buchanan-Adade sent me to live with Verne and Margaret Berry of Kalamazoo, Michigan, that state in the States where if you happen not to like the weather, all you have to do is to wait five minutes and it will change.

I had met the awesome couple of Margaret and Verne Berry in 1985 during their two-week visit with Tom to my Adade family in Togo. Supporting Tom's desire to send me to the States, the Berrys, a retired couple, were willing to show my Adade family their appreciation for our hospitality during their visit in Togo and host me at their home since Tom was living in Germany.

Such wonderful people—Tom Buchanan financed my two and a half years of education at Kalamazoo Valley Community College, and Margaret and Verne Berry provided me with free room and board.

My life with the Berrys was fun, memorable, enjoyable, and very nice. Verne, Margaret, and James, one of the Berrys' five kids, gave me all the love, attention, and everything that I needed to be happy and succeed in school. I still smile when I recall the countless jokes that Verne and his son, James, my other American brother after Tom Buchanan, and I used to enjoy, including one evening of fun when we had our pictures taken with the Hollywood actors of *Lethal Weapon*. In 1991, we met the two movies stars, Danny Glover and Mel Gibson, in a video store dumpster and used the giant promotional cutout for our photo session.

In December 1992, I graduated with an Associate's Degree in International Studies and Political Science and an academic record of being on the Dean's honor roll four times.

My decision to write these stories down in English, about one unique African family instead of in my national language of French is nothing less than my very personal way of saying thanks to Tom Buchanan, and my friends, the Berry family, my English instructor, Su Cutler, my dear mom Akoua, and dad Koffi Nicolas, my dear siblings Pauline. Fidel, and Jeanne, and, above all, my creator the Almighty God Jehovah for giving me this unique and unforgettable opportunity. Thank you all so very, very much, and may God bless you all.

About the Author

Pierre Komi T. Adadé was born in Agadji (Amou), a small farming community in Togo, West Africa. He attended a Catholic elementary school called Ecole Primaire St. Augustin of Agadji, College d'Enseignement General d'Agadji aka CEG of Agadji, College Protestant of Aneho, College St. Joseph of Lomé, Lycée de Tokoin of Lomé, University of Benin of Lome (aka University of Lome), and Kalamazoo Valley Community College (KVCC) in Kalamazoo, USA. He currently lives in Charlotte, North Carolina, USA. This book is a dedication to his father whose life story deserves to be shared with the whole world. The content of this book is well summarized in its title: *From an Orphan to Greatness: An African Story.* Enjoy his Journey!

CPSIA information can be obtained
at www.ICGtesting.com
Printed in the USA
JSHW081151240323
39413JS00001B/63